THE BLUEPRINT TO PERSONAL FINANCE FOR TEENS

8 Winning Steps to 10X Your Money Like a Pro by Learning How to Save, Invest, Budget, and Live Debt-Free

TAMMY FRANCIS

Copyright © 2024 Tammy Francis. All rights reserved.

The content within this book may not be reproduced, duplicated, or transmitted without direct written permission from the author or the publisher.

Under no circumstances will any blame or legal responsibility be held against the publisher, or author, for any damages, reparation, or monetary loss due to the information contained within this book, either directly or indirectly.

Legal Notice:

This book is copyright protected. It is only for personal use. You cannot amend, distribute, sell, use, quote, or paraphrase any part of the content within this book, without the consent of the author or publisher.

Disclaimer Notice:

Please note the information contained within this document is for educational and entertainment purposes only. All effort has been expended to present accurate, up-to-date, reliable, and complete information. No warranties of any kind are declared or implied. Readers acknowledge that the author is not engaged in the rendering of legal, financial, medical, or professional advice. The content within this book has been derived from various sources. Please consult a licensed professional before attempting any techniques outlined in this book.

By reading this document, the reader agrees that under no circumstances is the author responsible for any losses, direct or indirect, that are incurred as a result of the use of the information contained within this document, including, but not limited to, errors, omissions, or inaccuracies.

Contents

Acknowledgment	7
Your Journey Starts Here	9
1. STEP 1: ADULTING 101: THE "WHY"	13
Understanding Personal Finance: Budgeting and Investing	15
Reaching Self-Sufficiency	19
The Mindset for Financial Success	20
2. STEP 2: SAVINGS MADE EASY	25
Savings Equal Financial Freedom	26
Smart Decisions for Better Finances	28
How to Save Money	33
Savings Mistakes to Avoid	35
3. STEP 3: HOW TO USE CREDIT TO YOUR ADVANTAGE	39
Using Credit Wisely	42
What's in a Credit Score?	46
What's a Good Credit Score?	47
Good vs. Bad Debt	48
Common Mistakes to Avoid	50
4. STEP 4: THE WONDERFUL WORLD OF TAXES	55
How Does Tax Work?	56
Ask for Help!	58
Tax Mistakes to Avoid	60
5. STEP 5: BUDGETING: LIVING BELOW YOUR MEANS	65
Student Tips and Tricks	68
Pay Back Your Credit!	69
Why is Budgeting important?	73
Budgeting Techniques	73
Pitfalls To Avoid When Budgeting	75

6. STEP 6: MAKE MORE MONEY, REPEAT! 79
   Invest in Yourself 80
   Investment Opportunities 81
   Your Financial Journey 84
   Compounding Made Easy 88

7. STEP 7: THE SAVVY TEEN – SIDE HUSTLES 91
   "Hustling": What Does it Mean? 91
   Side Hustles Can Be Long-Term! 93
   Finding a Side Hustle 96
   Succeeding in Your Side Hustle 97

8. STEP 8: TIME MANAGEMENT 101
   Striking the Balance 102
   Lessons from the Swiss 104
   Prioritizing Self-Care 108
   Spotting the Signs of Burnout 111

   BONUS 1: FINANCIAL SAFETY 115
   Why Financial Safety Should Be on Your Radar 116
   Protecting Your Investments and All Things Legal 120
   The Takeaway 122

   BONUS 2: SELF-BRANDING FOR A HEALTHY
   FINANCIAL FUTURE 123
   Self-Branding and Financial Health 124
   Self-Branding, Step-By-Step 125
   The Do's and Don'ts of Self-Branding 127

   Conclusion and Next Steps 131
   References 133

It is with great honor that I dedicate this book to teens who need guidance in personal finance and are willing to start young to learn how to manage money smartly. I hope that what you are about to read inspires you to take action.

Acknowledgment

I am humbled and grateful to everyone who helped me create this book by putting in countless hours of editing and research material suggestions that seamlessly reinforced my points beautifully from the beginning to the end.

I am also thankful for the guidance and support from friends, family members, and mentors, who have taken the time out of their busy schedules to help me.

Your Journey Starts Here

Ah, the paradox of youth. You may be experiencing newfound financial independence by earning your own money for the first time. It is easy to find yourself overwhelmed by escalating expenses, as cash seems to slip through your fingers like sand. Questions abound: Are you spending to maintain a lifestyle you have grown accustomed to as a child? Are you attempting to dazzle your peers with the latest tech gadgets? Do you realize that you have been making significant purchases that consume a good chunk of your earnings while subsisting on a minimum wage?

From a seasoned professional who has traversed the realms of Real Estate and the corporate world, let me assure you that this confusion is familiar to your age group.

A staggering number of adults still need help grasping the concept of financial literacy. They may be managing their finances as best as possible or accepting that living pay cheque to pay cheque is the norm, but they often skate on thin ice simply because they need foundational knowledge. These gaps in understanding can be filled —provided we intentionally educate the younger generation.

Far from an old-fashioned lecture, this book aims to teach you through actionable steps. It is nice to feel that you have achieved your financial goals. The growing influence of social media often fuels an obsession with short-term gratification at the expense of long-term planning. The objective here is not to scold but to guide you away from these common pitfalls.

We live in a world increasingly dominated by extravagant experiences and trends, especially visible on social platforms. These spaces often amplify pressures that divert you from sensible financial practices toward impulsive spending. This is your wake-up call. Your opportunity to shift gears. It is a chance to adopt traits and habits that will help you navigate your remaining teenage years without constant financial anxiety and equip you with invaluable skills for adulthood.

This book serves as a roadmap for economic empowerment. Each chapter introduces critical concepts—from budgeting to investing—that can be game-changers for your financial health. Consider these chapters as building blocks designed to equip you with a solid grasp of managing, saving, and growing your money.

Your generation is vital to shaping the world of tomorrow. Adopting these essential skills is imperative for personal growth and societal progress. Financial literacy is not merely an individual pursuit; it equips you to contribute more meaningfully to the world around you.

I invite you to engage earnestly with the content herein. Whether you are reading this to get a handle on budgeting or as part of a broader endeavor to grasp financial fundamentals, the principles laid out will be instrumental, sooner or later. They may challenge your preconceived notions and even bewilder you sometimes. Still, each serves a crucial role in crafting a robust approach to financial literacy.

Take this journey seriously. Your future self will thank you for it.

Implementing and integrating these strategies will undoubtedly start you on the path to overcoming financial difficulties by creating a more wealthy and budget-oriented to-do list. Things may appear challenging since you have followed something and decided to do the opposite. Change is undoubtedly complex, but it is also highly flexible if you are susceptible to positive developments. If you need help focusing on what is essential, consider approaching it from a new angle, as you do by reading this book.

I have developed tactics to help you choose your financial goals based on all my work experience, from my first job to the present. I understand the worries that have grown for our youth. Everyone who reached the top has worked part-time at some point, earning an hourly wage while waiting tables or cooking meals. You must understand the big picture and really think about your future growth-oriented goals. The secret to resolving all of your issues is learning and adjusting!

I wish you the best in pursuing financial independence and effective budgeting. The tactics presented in this book will assist you in embarking on a fantastic adventure, enlighten you with fundamental notions, and help you to create the life you have always desired. You can continuously improve your life by making it your mission to seek knowledge and take action.

ONE

Step 1: Adulting 101: The "Why"

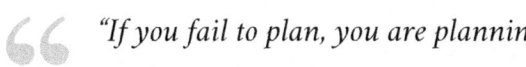 *"If you fail to plan, you are planning to fail."*

Benjamin Franklin

Having a plan is like a map guiding you in the right direction. Evaluating where you are now and where you need to go will help you succeed. Arming yourself with this knowledge will be essential to avoid the debt trap your parents' generation faced.

It is no secret that schools don't teach you about money. It is up to the parents to train the next generation about money, but how can most teach about money when they are not guided? This is where this book comes in handy. You are in a great position to learn because you have the gift of time on your side!

My observations in youth and finance have generally revealed two distinct categories. The first is a group of conscientious savers, young individuals who work diligently, tucking away most of their earnings for a largely undefined future. The second set comprises those driven by immediate desires—chasing the latest fashion trends, dining out, catching new film releases, or even spontaneous vacations. The burning question is: Which group are you a part of, and more importantly, what should you focus on?

The tendency to save scrupulously or spend impulsively isn't merely an individual quirk. Often, these are behaviors inherited from our families, deeply ingrained habits passed down from generation to generation. What would you inherit if financial wisdom—or lack thereof—were a family heirloom?

Robert Kiyosaki, a notable figure in financial education, once emphasized the necessity of "paying yourself first." He also encourages his readers to invest money instead of keeping it in the bank. Instead of formulating a budget around your expected expenditures and lifestyle desires, why not flip the script? Design your budget around your savings goals, centering the financial decisions you make today around the future you wish to secure. Doing so will cultivate a mindset that perpetually considers your long-term objectives. This shift is not merely fiscal but foundational, potentially influencing your financial wellness for the rest of your life.

You—the youth—are our assets and hope for the future. We harbor immense aspirations for your success. I want you to be inspired to forge a better world for yourself and future generations. For this to be accomplished, your financial enlightenment cannot be a deferred endeavor; it needs to begin here and now.

So, prepare for an enlightening voyage through the intricate landscapes of finance and budgeting. But this journey is not merely theoretical; it's intensely practical and profoundly impactful. It's not about quick fixes but enduring solutions that arm you with the skills to separate your 'wants' from your 'needs,' to prioritize your earnings in a manner that pays homage to your present self and future persona.

Start slowly, if you must. Incremental changes are better than none at all. With consistent effort and the right mindset, you will reach a point where your financial aspirations transform from mere figments of imagination into tangible reality.

Strap yourselves in; this will be an enriching ride through financial landscapes that can determine the quality of your life ahead. Your initiation into sensible budgeting and wise financial decisions begins now. The destination is worth the journey.

Understanding Personal Finance: Budgeting and Investing

Do you know what personal finance is? Specific nuances and details may appear confusing, but embrace learning with open arms. If you are unwilling to understand, you will experience failures that you will not be able to handle – we need to allow a loss to happen so we can overcome it. Nobody is born knowing everything, and not understanding specific processes or facts forces you to choose techniques that will not benefit you in the long run. Begin by understanding what personal finance is. Personal finance is about managing your money as efficiently and effectively as possible – knowing where it originates from and what it is used for.

I value this greatly because when you comprehend and know where money comes from, you will understand precisely how to spend it. For example, if you work eight hours a day earning minimum wage, you not only develop the skills you need for your future, but you also have an excellent baseline to develop the habit of saving and managing your money wisely because you will know the actual cost of your time.

Armed with this realization, working for a week or a month straight and then spending everything you have earned on things that might not make the most sense after a while, puts you on the defensive and forces you to deal with such scenarios. When you realize this, you will know you are on the right track: A route to achievement that will take time, but one day, you will have complete control.

Motivation is the second most crucial thing I want you to absorb. **"Today is your opportunity to build the tomorrow you want,"** by Ken Poirot, is a quote that perfectly expresses the passion and emphasis on this topic. Motivation goes a long way. If you are determined enough, you can even climb Mount Everest! Of course, motivation may not bring you to the top, but it will motivate you to pack your belongings and depart for the peak. This is what matters. It is critical to have a positive outlook. Staying motivated allows you to get out of bed in the morning.

It should be noted that motivation can only take you so far. It gets you out of bed in the morning, and discipline keeps you going. It ensures that you retain your wallet in your pocket and don't go on a spending spree. Be disciplined about what you do and how you do it.

Discipline breeds consistency. Consistency breeds results. This forces you to assess the opportunity cost and trade-off between what you must accomplish. For example, you may attend a meeting with your employers and know that if you outperform, you may get promoted. You will wake up motivated by the idea that you have to do it, and the day you obtain that promotion, you will understand that this is motivation.

Staying motivated will help you grasp the importance of working and achieving goals. A plan is critical since it motivates you to accomplish what you're working for. With determination, you will consider every penny you spend twice before purchasing. Any thrift transaction encourages financial incentives that may make you feel more fiscally conscious by having an excellent eye for detail and thinking twice before doing anything.

It is okay to treat yourself every now and again for doing well and sticking to the goals you have set for yourself. The idea is to stay motivated. Personal finance is all about managing your money coming in and going out. Don't spend more than you earn. Make a monthly budget and follow it strictly. Invest a portion of your savings. That's all you need to know about personal finances in a nutshell. But it is easier said than done. The biggest reason is a lack of motivation. To become motivated, we need to create a plan that enforces goals. Armed with a budgeting strategy is one of the most crucial financial habits you can develop and use. If this is your first time living on a budget and you have yet to see how beneficial it can be, it's easy to question why it's such a crucial component of personal finance. What do you desire the most? Is financial stability important? You can only attain the necessary consistency by including budgeting in every transaction.

By tracking spending and following a plan, a budget will force you to incur expenses while leaving you with enough finances to go through the rest of the week or month. Building an emergency fund, saving for major expenses and for the future, and saving for a car or a home may not seem so far-fetched.

I understand the origin of impulse purchases. Wearing fine clothing, going out for dinner, and having money in hand may make you feel great until you run out of money and have to live under the radar until your next paycheque arrives. This is due to a need for more planning. A budget may point you in the correct direction and force you to follow it to reach your objectives, spend within your means, and save for your education. Creating a budget does not have to be complicated. [1] People with less savings were more stressed out on average.

Investing a significant amount of your savings will propel you to reach your goals quickly. Investing may appear out-of-reach to you, or you may need clarification as to why you should even consider supporting this early in your life when you have a long future ahead. Investing at a young age will help you develop healthy financial habits and efficiently prepare you for the future. Even the tiniest amount of money saved through part-time employment, summer internships, family presents, or scholarship money could provide a head start and guide you through the marketplace, allowing you to take steps toward financial independence.

Developing a foundation to create a financially sound habit of saving most of your money before you mature into adulthood is for individuals of all ages because investing is an excellent method of putting money to work and producing a passive income, which will undoubtedly help you achieve financial freedom and a financially secure future.

Creating this thought pattern at an early age begins to methodically turn investments into wise investments. Inflation has hit an all-time high as the world's economy enters a critical phase. At the time of this writing, the economy has slowed, and wise investment will give the youth an advantage, allowing them to effectively time the market, outperform inflation, and gain value. By entering the market as soon as possible, you can create disciplined spending habits by focusing on your budget and decreasing costs as needed. The objective should always be to make money while saving money. However, this idea will only succeed if you have lousy spending habits and a life of impulsive purchases. The lesson from early investments will pay off in the long term, especially when you know you have nothing to worry about with passive income streaming.

Reaching Self-Sufficiency

Self-sufficiency is a feeling you can't imagine or feel unless you have felt it. It is like trying to think of a new color, which might feel impossible when you are young! And yet, that is what drives most young people towards financial literacy and financial freedom – independence. Dependence of any kind is not what you want for your future, as you do not wish to become a hindrance to yourself or others. Financial literacy is your gateway to freedom and accomplishment.

Since our existence began, humans have strived tirelessly to access resources. In the Neolithic period, they hunted for survival and grew crops. While people see these advancements as the evolution of human civilization, it could be argued, after a detailed analysis of psychology, economics, and history, that these were attempts to draw us further toward the goal of self-sustenance or self-sufficiency.

To draw an analogy as old as human history is to bring to light that these values are universal and still drive our decisions.

Being on top of your Personal finances aligns with these values and concepts. A penny earned through hard work gives you a more incredible feeling than if that money was handed to you.

These are perplexing times we live in. Despite living in the information age, the new generation must be more knowledgeable. Retiring on a 401K or any other retirement or pension fund and being financially free at 60 is no feat. I stress over the youth taking charge of their lives because the habits you instill when you are young yield results in the later years of your life.

Once you start learning about personal finance, you are already on a good path toward financial literacy. Take that knowledge and organize your finances. Set aside some money for savings, a little sum for your hobbies, and a tiny bit for buying a new phone. Show your parents the results of your decisions and then ask them for their feedback. If you have positive outcomes, then you're set.

These abilities cannot be developed in a traditional classroom setting. Budgeting skills must be practiced in real-world situations, so get working!

The Mindset for Financial Success

If one life skill remains conspicuously absent from the typical high school syllabus, it's financial literacy. You may be educated on algebra and history, but budgeting, investing, and understanding credit often need to be mentioned. As you read, having only some answers is perfectly fine. In fact, financial literacy isn't a sprint; it's a lifelong marathon. But what mindset should you adopt to stay ahead of the race?

Start Early, Stay Ahead

Firstly, dispel the notion that financial planning is a concern reserved for your future self. Time, as they say, is money. For young people, it is also a unique asset that you have in abundance. Whether saving a portion of your part-time job earnings, investing in a small way, or merely understanding how taxes work, the early bird catches the financial worm. The miracle of compound interest alone should be a compelling reason to not delay your introduction to the financial world. It's not just about having more years to save and invest; it's about letting your money work for you over time.

Curiosity Didn't Kill the Cat; It Made It Financially Savvy

Often, finances are reduced to mere numbers or transactional exchanges. But scratch beneath the surface, and you will find a multi-disciplinary arena that integrates psychology, sociology, and history. Curiosity might be the single most underrated trait regarding financial literacy. Go beyond just asking, "How much should I save?" and wonder, "Why do people find it hard to save in the first place?" or "How have economic policies evolved to impact individual financial decisions?" A curious mindset will challenge you to scrutinize conventional wisdom about money, equipping you to differentiate myths from hard facts.

A Dollar Today or a Nest Egg Tomorrow?

Being financially literate also demands a deep sense of responsibility. How you spend your money today echoes into your financial health tomorrow. The lattes and shoes might offer immediate gratification. Still, they don't contribute to your long-term goals like homeownership, education, or retirement. Yes, even at your age, retirement should be on your radar.

The ability to distinguish between 'needs' and 'wants' is an indispensable skill that tempers impulse buying with thoughtful decision-making. Your needs are non-negotiable and contribute to your well-being. Wants are the optional extras. Mastering balancing the two is like finding the financial philosopher's stone.

Building Resilience in the Financial Roller Coaster

It's naïve to think your financial journey will be smooth sailing. Whether your first investment is going awry or a budget plan has collapsed, setbacks are inevitable. But instead of perceiving them as failures, see them as your most invaluable teachers.

Financial resilience is not just about enduring the low moments; it's about learning from them to avoid future pitfalls.

Additionally, as the economic landscape changes due to technological advancements or global events, your resilience will guide you in adapting your strategies. You are not just surviving; you are evolving.

Knowledge Is Your Most Valuable Asset

Let's face it. The internet is flooded with advice, some good, but much of it is questionable. Be proactive but also discerning in what you choose to absorb. Read books on financial management by reputable authors, take online courses, or listen to podcasts, but always cross-reference the information you gather.

Better yet, seek mentorship from professionals or trusted adults who have demonstrated financial wisdom.

Engaging with your financial future is to be a lifelong student with a keen curiosity. Take charge with a high degree of responsibility, weather economic storms with unwavering resilience, and continually update your knowledge arsenal. This mindset won't just set you on the path to financial wellness. It will prepare you for the unpredictable journey that is life itself.

Remember that knowledge is useless without action. It is crucial to put into action what you have learned so that you can begin benefiting from the knowledge right away.

TWO

Step 2: Savings Made Easy

 "Never spend your money before you've earned it."

Thomas Jefferson

When you first enter the world of work, planning out what you will spend and save is essential. It is easy to get trapped in the web of impulsive purchases when you could save this money and use it for more critical things later. This would include wiser decisions and likely result in fulfillment from defining and attaining financial objectives. In other words, you must know the difference between short-term enjoyment and long-term planning and budgeting. It helps to create a chart to list your goals and divide them into two categories. Short-term objectives should include buying a new phone, saving for a vacation, or paying off a debt. Long-term objectives should consist of whatever you desire for the long term. Do you want a car? You need to save up for it, which might mean skipping a few short-term sources of enjoyment!

Do you aim to create a better and more stable financial future? Join the bandwagon as what I am about to say will enlighten you about financial budgeting and saving. We focus more on the traditional ideas of saving pennies in piggy banks, which we used to do when discussing saving money. Over time, various creative options emerged and have changed and transformed. Managing your finances and savings includes allowing your money to grow rather than spending it, for example, as you are young, you can benefit much from saving since you have more time to increase your savings the sooner you learn to do so.

Savings Equal Financial Freedom

It should be no surprise that teens spend a substantial portion of their income due to the convenience of online shopping.[1] In fact, shoppers aged between 13-to-18 years old spent twice the rate of adults, and shop online twice as much as adults!. Specifically, online purchases accounted for 17.9% of transactions. Video games represented 39.3%, with streaming online services representing 14.6% of online spending. The remaining 46% were a more traditional mix of consumer goods, including clothing, cosmetics, novelty items and accessories.

The youth frequently splurge all their money immediately on things that make them happy. However, they must grasp that every dollar they spend reduces their ability to save for future goals.

[2]According to Harvard professor Gerald Zaltman, 95% of purchasing decisions are subconscious. Emotional responses to financial purchases need the appropriate brake mechanism so that they do not lead to overspending and push you to purchase much more than you would in a brick-and-mortar establishment. It is crucial to step in early to set yourself on the proper financial track

as soon as possible because this spendthrift conduct might foretell disastrous financial decisions later in your life!

I am very critical of the whole spendthrift and impulsive buying phenomenon. However, we have grown accustomed to the circumstances and the situations that lead us to do this. Using these methods in this book effectively develops the success habits you can use throughout your life that will bring you to your objectives quicker.

You can start to edit the things you want but do not need. For example, if you receive an ad for a newer phone with a deal to entice you to upgrade, discern and assess if the upgrade is worth the extra cost or if you can keep using your existing phone to save the additional cost.

The sooner you understand how to distinguish between needs and wants, the sooner you can reduce spending. Learning how to put off gratification and think through your purchasing decisions is essential.

I will share a simple method with you that is easy to incorporate. Since there is no cap on spending power, I frequently asked myself, **"Would I rather save a lot of money by dining at home or going out with my friends?"** I used to convince myself that walking two or three blocks was preferable to taking the bus or a taxi. This was challenging at times, but these challenges pale compared to the prospect of living the life of your dreams and building the future you have always wanted. Even though the future looked far away then, the most important thing was to try.

Smart Decisions for Better Finances

You don't have to sacrifice everything today in favor of the future; you only need to make intelligent decisions. Spending money on needs can't make you feel bad.

For instance, you should buy a new laptop if you require one for your studies or to generate money. If a $500 laptop can do jobs for you flawlessly, you may not need to spend $1,000 on a computer. That is just thrifty spending! It's the attitude that counts, and constancy is what should win out.

Be careful with uncontrolled spending. Uncontrolled spending is when you buy something extra at the checkout that was not on your list. Have you ever noticed that in the lineup at the store, there are all these cute little easy-grab items? Stores place those items strategically to satisfy impulse spending.

Not having a plan before going to a store makes you susceptible to compulsive shopping and spending if left unchecked. This mentality about money might cause you to spend more than you can comfortably afford.

Short-term and long-term savings go hand in hand

Understanding that you must have a specific objective in mind for what you want to do with your money is crucial for your success. Saving up will only make sense if you have a goal. If you don't have any plans or goals, it's nearly a given that you will get off course and spend all of your funds eventually. It is encouraged to develop good financial habits rooted in place before saving money. What are you saving for, and how much would best achieve your objectives?

[3]The power of habit is almost as important as the power of time when it comes to money. Developing healthy habits takes discipline, but it is wise to put it into practice to become automatic. Once it is

automated, this good habit will be with you even into adulthood. After determining what to save for, it's time for some arithmetic and planning. Determine your income, whether from a job, an allowance, or anything else.

Learn the skills of banking and saving to determine how much money would be required to spend each month on basics.

Since we have been discussing finance and budgeting throughout, it's necessary to clarify the idea of banking. Banking is the commercial activity of receiving, securing, and lending out money that belongs to other people or companies to carry out economic activities like creating a profit or merely paying for operational costs. Numerous financial organizations that store the money of people, corporations, and other entities are included in banking. Banks offer financial services that assist in managing, investing, and saving money. Why is this significant? Because those who are underbanked cannot use services that promote economic security. You can use services outside the banking system to cash checks or borrow money, resulting in more significant transaction costs and unnecessary interest.

Banking is a great way to start out, as it trains you to save money. You should immediately open a bank account if you are dedicated and work shifts around the clock.

Why so? Think about it this way. If you have cash on hand with whatever you earn, there will probably come a time when you get off track and spend too much. This is because, to start with, you can't just stash up cash or dig up grounds to store your earnings because you will most definitely be drawn to it. Also, there are no benefits to keeping money in your house.

You will quickly realize that your wealth and money are just building up and your savings are increasing, and you will likely ask yourself if spending the extra $50 on a new jacket or a fancy lunch is worthwhile. Therefore, now is the ideal moment to increase your knowledge of banking, investing, and budgeting to increase your income.

Banking promotes a strong sense of self-accountability and is a good practice for adulthood. Understandably, you might still depend on your parents to fund your needs and want to manage your expenses. With a bank account, you would be more self-reliant in managing your money. If you have banking insights, you could closely monitor your spending. You won't always be a teenager and will eventually have to deal with more challenging duties that might cause you to buckle under the strain if you don't prepare for them.

Understanding the many forms of banking accounts will give you the edge you need to make effective decisions. Roth IRA (tax-free savings accounts), savings accounts, and chequing accounts exist. The most popular kind of account globally is the chequing account. It is the preferred account for most individuals because of how simple operations, such as cash withdrawals and deposits, are made for its members.

To open a regular chequing account in the U.S., one must be at least 18.

The interest rates are lower because chequing accounts are not meant to hold funds for lengthy periods or compounding. One can put money in a savings account for compounding, but we will get to that later.

Chequing accounts are primarily utilized to store cash for daily transactions. Do you intend to pay the bills the following week? The money should remain in the chequing account. Do you desire to purchase a new pair of shoes? Place your funds in a chequing account. The chequing account's unrestricted deposit capacity is another essential feature. It is often suggested that large sums should not be put in the chequing account.

For instance, depositing funds in the chequing account is not wise if a parent is trying to save money to pay for their child's college expenses.

Examining the savings account comes second. When you consider saving, what comes to mind? Scratch that. What does it mean when your mother tells you to save pocket money? We can better understand by studying the exact opposite to understand the whole picture. This applies to chequing and savings accounts. On one end is the savings account. A savings account is going west if a chequing account is heading east. It saves money. Your chequing account is different from this one. It could, however, be connected to your chequing account. The cash you put here has a greater interest rate than a chequing account and is susceptible to compounding. People who desire to store money for a rainy day might use this account. It should be emphasized that it is optional to do it for a significant reason. Most people save money in a savings account for future investments. They consider it a safe way to increase their fortune because many individuals are risk-averse.

A savings account also provides liquidity but slightly less flexibility than a standard chequing account. A sizable portion of your money is protected an additional benefit of putting your money in a savings account.

Take a quick look at the Roth IRA (Individual Retirement Account). American banks offer Roth IRA accounts. The main advantage is that it is tax-free, and you can withdraw your earnings tax-free and penalty-free once the account has been open for at least five years.

This is a good savings option as you set yourself up for your future when you expect to be in a higher tax bracket.

No, there aren't any unstated expenses in a Roth IRA. It is tax-free, and you pay no taxes on any profits or interest you earn. Since practically everything in today's society is subject to taxation, I understand that you may find this strange. No money from your Roth IRA withdrawal will be sent to the government. The Roth IRA is a plan for those who want to gain money over an extended period.

In contrast, the ordinary savings account is for short- to medium-term holding. High-net-worth individuals with a far more varied portfolio than others now frequently use it. This enables individuals to relieve the tension from high taxes, strict regulations, and other monetary concerns. Most Americans consider the Roth IRA essential for their retirement planning because of its success and benefit to investors. If you are 18 or older, open a chequing account first. Be willing to maintain a savings account if you have a propensity for financial planning. Use the chequing account for all your regular banking requirements and the savings account for any excess money. Open a Roth IRA later in your career when you have a reliable income source and want to add other streams through investments.

Play the long game and do so shrewdly. The road to financial security and independence is long and taxing. Still, with careful planning, you can travel it without incident. Continue to learn more about the many possibilities and alternatives available.

I encourage you to develop the critical qualities needed to hit the ground running. Less in the capacity of a mentor and more in the power of a friend. You should make better consumption selections and find fulfillment in creating and attaining the predetermined financial objectives. Saving money should be necessary since it is the fundamental building block to realizing your dream of economic freedom. If your parents don't have an endless supply of income, trying to find independence and comfort might be difficult at such a young age. Learning the foundations will thus prevent you from experiencing any unpleasant shocks in the future.

Go for everything that can provide you a better foundation, more equity, or a more diverse portfolio. You can feel hesitant and like you're lost in the Cornfield maze.

Remember the words of the great Gonzo journalist Hunter Thompson, *"Never turn your back on fear. It should always be in front of you, like a thing that might have to be killed."*

How to Save Money

First let's acknowledge a simple truth. Money is more than paper and coins. It's the means to freedom, choice, and comfort. In essence, money is a tool that can be wielded wisely or foolishly, and the best part is that you get to decide how to use it. You don't have to be a Wall Street whiz kid or a math prodigy to understand the basics of saving. All it takes is the right mindset and some innovative strategies.

Start Simple: The Piggy Bank Method

You have likely had a piggy bank or some sort of jar where you stash away coins and small bills. But have you thought of it as your first savings account? While it might seem rudimentary, even archaic, physically putting money into a container provides a tangible sense of saving. Once your piggy bank is complete, take it to a savings account. That brings us to our next point.

Level Up: The Bank Savings Account

Most banks offer savings accounts specifically tailored for young people. Opening one is an educational experience in itself. You learn about interest rates, minimum balances, and the joy of seeing your money grow over time. If you're under 18, you will need a parent or guardian to co-sign, but make sure your name is associated with the account. This is your journey, after all.

The Power of Compounding

Albert Einstein famously called compound interest the "eighth wonder of the world." What is it? Imagine you start with $100 in your savings account, and it earns an interest rate of 5% per year. After one year, you will have $105. But in the second year, you make interest not just on your original $100 but also on the $5 interest from the first year. Over time, this effect snowballs, turning small, consistent contributions into a sizable sum. Start young, and give yourself more time to let this wonder work wonders on your savings.

Divide and Conquer: The Bucket Strategy

Not all savings are created equal. You can save for short-term goals like buying a new game, medium-term goals like an incredible summer camp, or long-term plans like college. Create separate 'buckets' for each purpose. You can do this virtually through different accounts or sub-accounts or by keeping multiple piggy banks. By segmenting your savings, you can better track your progress and prioritize. You can name each savings account as the thing you are saving for. For example, your "Vacation" fund is separate from your "Clothing" fund.

Involve Your Parents: The Match Program

Get your parents invested in your savings plan. Propose a match program where they match a percentage of what you save. For instance, they might contribute fifty cents for every dollar you save. Not only does this accelerate your savings, but it also instills a sense of shared purpose and responsibility.

Boost Your Income: Odd Jobs and Side Hustles

Saving doesn't mean you have to skimp on every pleasure. Think about how you can expand your income. Can you mow lawns, pet-sit, or help neighbors with errands? These small earnings can supplement your savings without compromising your lifestyle.

Savings Mistakes to Avoid

Thomas Jefferson once said, *"Never spend your money before you have earned it,"* and he couldn't be more right!

Some mistakes are commonly made when saving, so let's look at them.

The Siren Song of Instant Gratification

The most prevalent trap that snares young savers is the allure of instant gratification.

With the world at your fingertips, literally through smartphones, it's tempting to splurge on the latest trends or tech gadgets. However, giving in to these impulses can quickly deplete your savings. The fix? Before making any purchase, give yourself a cooling-off period to evaluate whether you truly need the item or if it's just a fleeting desire.

Underestimating Small Expenses

We will discuss those $5 coffees or the enticing in-app purchases in your favorite mobile game. They seem insignificant, don't they? Well, they're not. Small expenditures have a way of adding up quickly, eroding your savings without you even realizing it. The best way to combat this is by tracking your spending. Various apps are designed to do just that, or you could go old-school and jot down everything in a notebook. You would be surprised how much you can save by cutting out or cutting back on these seemingly minor expenses.

Ignoring the Power of Compound Interest

You may make the mistake of stashing your savings in a drawer or under a mattress. While this might keep your money 'safe,' it doesn't allow it to grow. Banks offer interest on savings accounts, and the earlier you start, the more time your money has to grow through compound interest. Don't discount this as something only adults need to worry about; this is a long game, and starting young gives you a head start.

Saving Without Specific Goals

While saving money just for saving is commendable, this approach needs more direction and can lead to consistent savings habits. Instead, aim to save with specific goals in mind. Whether for a car, college, or even a cool new gadget, having a target can make the process more rewarding and provide a tangible sense of achievement.

Mixing Savings and Chequing Accounts

If you have a chequing account, keeping all your funds in one place for convenience can be tempting. This, however, can blur the lines between what you can spend and what you should save. Open a separate savings account and rigorously move a set percentage of your income or allowance there. Consider this account a one-way street: Money goes in but doesn't come out, except for emergencies or planned expenditures.

Neglecting Financial Education

You may have opened a savings account, but do you know about other investment options like stocks, bonds, or mutual funds? Your teen years are still early enough to start learning about these. [4]Research indicates that the financial literacy of U.S. teens is low, yet they have access to and spend a great deal of money each year. Teens were surveyed in 1998 and again in 2008 to determine what teens wanted to know about money and how they wanted to learn. The findings indicate that teens are still interested in learning about many of the same financial topics identified in 1998, but their desire for web education has increased. The lack of financial education can lead to poor decisions later in life. So, take the initiative: There are countless resources available, from books to online courses, that can turn you into a savvy investor well before you reach adulthood. And yes, this book is part of this!

Listening to Peer Pressure

Finally, remember that your financial journey is yours. It is not a group project. Peer pressure to spend on things you don't need can be intense at this age. If your friends are all buying designer clothes or the latest smartphones, the urge to fit in can derail your savings plan. But keep your eye on the bigger picture; the discipline you instill now will set the stage for financial freedom as an adult.

Saving money as a teen is a worthy endeavor that can determine the course of your financial future. But like any journey, it comes with challenges and pitfalls. By being aware of these potential mistakes and taking proactive steps to avoid them, you can ensure that your path to financial wellness remains unobstructed. Remember, foresight and discipline are more valuable than any windfall in personal finance!

THREE

Step 3: How to Use Credit to Your Advantage

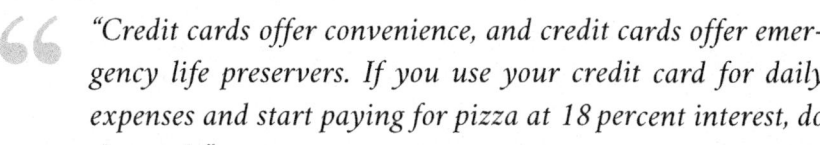 *"Credit cards offer convenience, and credit cards offer emergency life preservers. If you use your credit card for daily expenses and start paying for pizza at 18 percent interest, do the math."*

Ed Mierzwinski

Once upon a time, in a suburban town, Jamie was an 18-year-old fresh out of high school and ready to seize the world. Jamie was a popular figure in school, known for always having the latest gadgets, the trendiest clothes, and the most fantastic accessories.

As Jamie entered adulthood, the magic ticket arrived—a credit card approval letter with a whopping $5,000 limit.

"Imagine all the stuff I can buy now!" Jamie thought gleefully.

For the first few months, life was a shopping spree. Online carts filled up like magic, and the doorstep was a parade of delivery packages. Friends marveled at Jamie's latest iPhone, designer bags, and a brand-new gaming console.

"Wow, Jamie, you're so lucky to afford all this," they would say.

"Ah, it's nothing," Jamie would reply with a smug grin, never revealing the plastic secret in the wallet.

Soon enough, the credit card bill arrived. The minimum payment seemed doable, so Jamie paid it off, ignoring the remaining balance and the interest rates—terms that felt like financial jargon from another universe.

Weeks turned into months, and the buying continued, but the credit card bill became a looming monster. The minimum payment grew, and Jamie started missing them, thinking, "How bad could it be?"

Then, one day, Jamie wanted to buy a car. With no proper understanding of credit scores, Jamie walked into the dealership only to face rejection after the credit check.

"Sorry, we can't approve your loan. Your credit score is far too low," the dealer said, his expression on his face was a mix of pity and disbelief.

"Credit score? What's that?" Jamie asked.

The dealer explained that a credit score measures financial responsibility, and Jamie's excessive use of credit without paying it back had tanked the score.

Confused and alarmed, Jamie went home and researched.

A low credit score could affect everything—loan approvals, renting apartments, and even job applications. It was a record of your financial reliability, and Jamie's record was terrible.

Things spiraled quickly from there. The unpaid credit card bills turned into a debt collection notice, the phone kept ringing with creditors' calls, and Jamie was sinking into a pit of anxiety and regret.

After a consultation with a financial advisor, Jamie was given a grim solution—filing for bankruptcy.

For those who don't know, bankruptcy is a legal process that allows individuals or businesses who cannot pay their debts to seek relief from some or all of their debts.

Simply put, it's a way to say, "I can't handle this debt. Please help me start over." But this fresh start comes at a steep price. Bankruptcy stays on your credit report for up to 10 years, making future borrowing expensive or impossible. Plus, not all types of debts are cleared through bankruptcy; student loans, for instance, are hard to shake off.

With no other option left, Jamie filed for bankruptcy. The court examined Jamie's finances and concluded that repaying this debt was impossible. Some of Jamie's debt was wiped clean, but their credit history was back to square zero, like a game of financial snakes and ladders.

Jamie had to start anew, this time learning the basics of financial literacy—budgeting, saving, and understanding credit. The bankruptcy offered a hard reset, but the lesson was harsher.

Years passed, and while Jamie's friends moved on with their lives—getting cars, houses, and steady jobs—Jamie was still playing catch-up, a pariah in the credit world.

Finally, a decade later, the bankruptcy label was lifted off Jamie's credit report. It had been a long, arduous journey back to financial normalcy. Now older and wiser, Jamie advocated for financial literacy, especially among young people.

"I wish someone had told me how dangerous credit can be if not used responsibly," Jamie would say to anyone who'd listen, especially teenagers like you who are about to embark on their own financial journeys.

The moral of the story is that credit is not free money; it's a responsibility. Treat it with the respect it deserves, or face a long, uphill battle to regain your financial standing. And remember, sometimes the most challenging life lessons come from mistakes we didn't even know we were making. But don't worry – this is what this chapter will teach you.

Using Credit Wisely

A credit card goes a long way in terms of an efficient and practical approach to establishing a good credit score. As we get older, our lives are greatly influenced by having a solid credit history from a young age. It goes without saying that having access to a credit card helps you navigate toward achieving financial independence!

I have simplified things for my readers who need help understanding credit cards by listing a few fundamentals everyone should know. In essence, a credit card is a facility that allows customers access to funds up to a pre-set and pre-approved credit limit. Simply said, you may always use your credit card to make a purchase if you are short on cash. However, you'll have to make up the difference when the bank sends you a credit history statement the following month, plus any applicable interest and additional agreed-upon charges, either in full by the billing date or over.

A credit card is more than just a piece of plastic and may be essential in helping you stabilize your financial situation. In credit cards and banking, making responsible purchases and paying them off on time creates the most vital item: credit history. It is based on various practices, including regular, on-time payments, avoiding late fees, maintaining a low debt-to-income ratio, and keeping credit use below the credit limit.

There is no question that when you become older and develop a strong credit history, you will eventually be able to obtain loans if you combine these methods in the best possible way. Essentially, the score is determined by evaluating the likelihood that a borrower would repay a loan.

The borrower seems more creditworthy to the lender when their credit ratings are higher, which increases their ability to access credit. Starting as early as possible is vital since building and maintaining a solid credit score over time can take time and effort. The procedure may move soon for those with a large sum of money in their bank accounts, but for those who make only a few hundred or thousand dollars a month, things might take some time.

You should obtain credit cards as soon as possible to achieve the highest levels of monetary security by the time you are older. There are some benefits connected to the idea that, once you learn about them, considering them and choosing them would make perfect sense. For instance, did you realize that acquiring a credit card will make tracking your financial situation much easier? By checking your credit score and report, you may learn more about your financial situation and what else needs to be on your priority list. The credit report generated entails past and present credit transactions. By checking it regularly, you can identify any errors or discrepancies that may lower your score.

Let's think about it this way as well. In a hypothetical situation, you would have achieved financial independence over time and paid for all your educational costs up to high school. Since opening a bank account as soon as you turn 18 and putting up all your wages would give you a strong credit score, you might not even need to worry about your college tuition. This is why having a credit history could be helpful. A solid credit history would assist someone who pays for their education independently.

Now that you all understand what a credit score is and why it is important let's talk about how a high credit score may be beneficial in the long term. Imagine that you have been putting money aside since you were a teenager to buy the car of your dreams. Assume you only have enough money to cover the down payment on a vehicle. Still, the bank will be okay covering the remaining balance if you have a strong credit score and a credit history showing on-time payments.

You can be eligible for better credit cards with a strong credit score. Note that not all credit cards are created equal. Diamond, Gold, and Platinum credit cards are the most widely utilized, so you have probably heard of the terms. You must have a solid and exceptional credit history to qualify for these categories and receive rewards or other premium perks. Some credit card rewards programs even give out hundreds of dollars in cash back or bonuses. They also provide cardholders loyalty points they may use to get a free night's stay at a five-star hotel.

What do you want to accomplish in the following five years? Do you want to own your private business or work for someone else? What if I told you that a strong credit score is crucial in these sectors? Have you ever wondered how much a strong credit score might contribute to a person's identity? Surprised, right? When you apply for a job, your potential employer might quickly check your credit history. You are undoubtedly perplexed about why your next boss needs to know your credit history. It is important to note that having a decent credit score speaks to your trustworthiness and demonstrates that the applicant is a true professional who handles daily activities responsibly.

One of the essential qualities an employer looks for in a candidate is responsibility. Lousy credit may indicate that you don't keep your word and don't care about committing to something. The same is true if you own a business since you could require money or a loan from a bank to get by. Still, suppose you don't keep your promises. In that case, nobody will trust you in the market—not the banks or individual investors. Speaking about private investors, they look into your records before deciding to partner with your company to see if you have any liabilities you could be utilizing their money for, and that's when they choose to back out of partnerships.

Even if you don't want to buy a home, you may be required to rent one, which requires a solid credit rating. Many individuals must realize that your landlord would take your credit score seriously when reviewing your rental application. Since a history of on-time payments considerably impacts the landlord's choice to provide the property to you as a tenant rather than someone filled out with delinquencies, you are more likely to receive that place if your credit report and scores show good numbers.

As for insurance, you won't necessarily need to apply for it— whether for a car, health, or anything else—until you turn eighteen. Since your parents have been taking care of the insurance up to this point, I can assure you that when you become an adult and start seeing a significant portion of your income go toward insurance, you will find it perplexing. Research, however, suggests that credit ratings can aid in predicting insurance losses. [1]People with less than stellar credit histories *on average* file more insurance claims than those with stellar credit histories. This correlation has been repeatedly validated. Maintaining an excellent credit score enables you to support affordable vehicle and health insurance premiums and would also keep your reputation favorable in the eyes of your insurance provider.

What's in a Credit Score?

Now that I have explained the benefits a good credit history holds, let's shed some light on how to build a good credit history. As discussed earlier, making a good credit history depends on various practices, including regular, on-time payments, avoiding late fees, maintaining a low debt-to-income ratio, and keeping credit use below the credit limit.

First, you may enter the world of credit cards and banking by getting one or more starter cards, depending on how much you require. Your credit score and credit ratings will instantly increase if you have one or more credit cards you use to pay off your bills on time. It will help you and the bank establish a solid reputation, eventually leading to better interest rates and more significant daily transaction limits. Did you know that Shaquille O'Neil once used his credit card to make purchases totaling $70,000 at Walmart? The bank had to contact him in case his card had been stolen. Do you now understand how good a connection with the bank and such significant transaction limits feels? You will eventually gain a lot more confidence from the banks and be able to qualify for other types of loans, such as mortgages, that you might need in the next five years when you plan to settle down once you have proven your abilities and incorporated qualities that depict timely and consistent payments.

Using your accounts properly and paying them off monthly

Lenders have greater market power than borrowers. Lenders want to see people follow through on their promises. Therefore, it is very beneficial if someone has a payment history before requesting more considerable sums. Take my advice: establishing excellent credit takes time and may be difficult for some of you. I have a guide you can easily follow and will encourage you to spend at most 30% of your available credit on your credit cards.

Please be aware and ensure that you will harm your credit score and reputation with each missed payment or maxed-out card. Consider the shame you would have if you handed the cashier your credit card, which he returned to you, claiming it is maxed out. A bright tip is to budget and manage your spending appropriately by setting up automated payment systems. By planning your expenses ahead of time, you may avoid any difficulty in the long run. In this manner, ensure you always have the funds to pay your payments.

What's a Good Credit Score?

Even though ratings greatly depend on credit score ranges, credit ratings between 580 and 669 are generally considered fair. Good credit scores are those between 670 and 739, while credit scores fall between 740 and 799, which is very good. Anything beyond 800 is exceptional and will increase your chances of building a stellar credit history.

These are just a few things you need to start working on early enough because something as simple as a credit history might need to be clarified for people of your age, but where we sit today, having a good credit history plays a pivotal role. This message is directed to my readers who someday want to become successful and reach the top.

Good vs. Bad Debt

In an era where financial jargon is often tossed around casually, the term "debt" almost universally provokes anxiety and apprehension. Society has taught us to associate debt with adverse outcomes, from bankruptcy to financial ruin. However, this perception oversimplifies the nuanced reality of debt. In fact, not all debt is created equal. Understanding the difference between "good debt" and "bad debt" can be pivotal in financial planning and, more broadly, in navigating the labyrinth of personal finance.

What Constitutes Good Debt?

Good debt can be likened to an investment: you borrow capital to fuel future growth, whether personal, educational, or financial. Good debt can increase your net worth or add long-term value to your life.

Take student loans, for example. The idea of owing tens of thousands of dollars before entering the workforce can be daunting. However, a college degree often leads to higher earning potential and broader career opportunities. If managed wisely, this debt can be a stepping stone to a more prosperous future.

Another example is a mortgage for a home. While a mortgage is a long-term commitment, homeownership has its own financial advantages, including potential tax benefits and home equity. The goal is to own an asset that appreciates over time, ultimately enhancing your financial standing.

The Pitfalls of Bad Debt

Bad debt can be described as borrowing money to purchase depreciating assets or consumables. These expenses offer no long-term benefit and can erode your financial health. Credit card debt accrued from lifestyle inflation, such as buying the latest gadgets or designer clothes, falls squarely into this category. [2]The interest rate that your credit card charges you makes a difference. Many credit cards can charge as much as 29% on unpaid balances. High-interest rates can prevent you from paying down your debt. The high-interest rates that come with credit card debt can trap you in a vicious cycle of ever-increasing financial obligations.

Similarly, payday loans are a quintessential example of bad debt. Although this may appear attractive initially, they are designed to provide quick cash. These loans come with exorbitant interest rates.

People who rely on payday loans often find themselves in a perpetual debt loop, further diminishing their economic well-being.

A Balanced Perspective

Understanding that the binary classification of good and bad debt is not absolute. It is crucial. Context matters. A mortgage can become bad debt if the home value plummets or you can no longer afford the monthly payments. Conversely, a car loan is generally considered bad debt because cars depreciate rapidly—it could be justified if it enables you to accept a higher-paying job that you otherwise couldn't reach.

The key is to assess the long-term impact of your borrowing decisions. Before taking on any debt, consider the interest rates, the monthly payments, and most importantly, your capacity to repay. Always ask yourself: will this debt improve my life in a meaningful, long-term way, or will it just offer short-term gratification at the expense of my future financial security?

Empowering Through Knowledge

Understanding the nuances of good and bad debt empowers us to make informed decisions that align with our financial goals and life circumstances. Mastering this concept early on is invaluable. It lays the groundwork for financial literacy, ensuring that when faced with life's pivotal moments—college, buying a home, or even starting a business—they are equipped to make choices that will serve them well in the long run.

In a society that often views debt through a monolithic lens, differentiating between good and bad debt is an essential life skill. This isn't just financial wisdom; it's a form of self-awareness that transcends dollars and cents, equipping you with the discernment to make life choices that either propel you forward or hold you back. Choose wisely.

Common Mistakes to Avoid

As you are just entering the world of personal finance, the concept of a credit score may seem nebulous. But make no mistake: This three-digit number can impact pivotal life decisions, from buying a car to renting an apartment and even job opportunities. As someone who has been through the financial trenches and emerged wiser, I find learning to manage credit wisely early is invaluable. Here is where a lot of people tend to go astray.

Ignoring the Importance of Credit

You might think, "I'm too young to worry about credit." But the sooner you start building it, the better. A more extended credit history contributes positively to your credit score. Ignoring this early on puts you at a disadvantage when you need good credit for more significant financial moves.

Applying for Multiple Credit Cards Simultaneously

You can sign up for several credit cards as soon as you're eligible, especially when enticing offers come through the mail or are pushed at store counters, but you must be cautious. Each application results in a "hard inquiry" on your credit report, which could reduce your score. Multiple inquiries suggest to lenders that you might be a high-risk customer.

Maxing Out Your Credit Card

Credit cards aren't a ticket to unlimited spending. In fact, the best practice is to use less than 30% of your available credit limit. Maxing out your card sends a red flag to credit bureaus, showing you might be financially irresponsible.

Making Late Payments

If there's one thing you take away from this chapter, let it be this: Always pay your bills on time. Even a single late payment can damage your credit score and remain on your credit report for up to seven years. Set reminders or automate payments to ensure you get all the due dates.

Ignoring Your Credit Report

Many young people don't even glance at their credit reports because this is often not a thought that comes to mind. However, mistakes happen. Incorrect information could be affecting your score without you knowing it. You're entitled to an annual free credit report from the three main credit bureaus. Use them.

Closing Old Accounts

You may think closing an old or unused credit card is responsible. However, this can backfire by shortening your credit history, reducing your available credit, and hurting your credit score. Keep those old accounts open, but manage them wisely.

Falling for Quick Fixes

If you have a low credit score, there's no magic wand to wave and make it better overnight.

Companies that promise to do so are likely scams. Rebuilding credit takes time and disciplined financial behavior.

Not Having a Diverse Credit Mix

While you shouldn't borrow just for diversifying, having different types of credit—like a credit card, a student loan, or a retail account—can improve your score. Lenders like to see that you can handle various types of credit responsibly.

Co-Signing Loans for Friends

Co-signing is a helpful gesture but comes with risks. If the person you co-signed for fails to make timely payments, your credit score will be hit. Steer clear of co-signing unless you can fully trust the other party to manage the loan responsibly.

Ignoring Financial Literacy

Your financial education should be learned through something other than trial and error. Plenty of resources are available that teach the ins and outs of credit scores, interest rates, and budgeting. Use them.

Your credit history is crucial and laden with potential pitfalls. Yet, it's also ripe with opportunities for setting the stage for a stable financial future. As young people on the cusp of many significant life events—college, first jobs, independence—it's imperative to take the reins of your financial health now.

Building credit is a marathon, not a sprint, and the race starts long before you're pondering mortgages and retirement funds. Start strong, avoid these mistakes, and you'll be miles ahead in the long run.

"Your Credit Score affects the interest rates you're offered on credit cards and loans, can be used to vet your job application, and in some states may influence your insurance premiums."

Suze Orman

Here is an interesting poll that highlights the average debt balance by age group:

[3]Gen Z (ages 18 to 23): $9,593

- Millennials (ages 24 to 39): $78,396
- Gen X (ages 40 to 55): $135,841
- Baby boomers (ages 56 to 74): $96,984
- Silent generation (ages 75 and above): $40,925

According to Experian, consumers in the two oldest age categories have seen a significant decrease in debt since 2015 (about -7.5% for baby boomers and -7.7% for the silent generation overall).

The article provides a breakdown of the indebtedness for each group. The Gen X group had the highest debt: credit card debt, auto loans, student loans, and mortgage loans. Baby boomers had the highest personal loan debt. Millennials had the most significant debt increase from 2015 to the present, and Gen Z had the lowest debt compared to the other groups but struggled to make payments.

The reality is that most people will carry debt through to their retirement. This is not to scare you, but to be made aware of the facts of not having financial literacy and taking action from a young age will give you the boost you need for success.

FOUR

Step 4: The Wonderful World of Taxes

 "The hardest thing in the world to understand is the income tax."

Albert Einstein

Taxes! Yes, it's time to clarify the idea of taxes and provide some insightful ideas that were crucial when I was young.

This helps you realize what you must do to manage your money successfully.

Tax is a mandatory payment you need to pay on any income you get, such as business earnings, or is frequently added to the items you purchase on the open market and other commodities, services, or transactions.

In other words, the amount you must contribute each year is determined by your income or the value of your home.

The term "tax," which is short for "taxation," includes direct and indirect taxes. The implementation and rules governing the two are different. For instance, certain taxes must be paid directly, like income taxes, while others may be paid indirectly, like sales taxes.

There are two kinds of taxes; direct and indirect taxes. A direct tax is the kind of tax that must be paid to the government immediately. It cannot be transferred to another party or made to be paid on your behalf by someone else. The one who has been personally assessed with it must bear it. Income taxes can be an example of direct taxes. Income taxes are calculated based on the user's money and annual income. It is a direct tax since those who pay it are likely responsible for paying it back. However, indirect taxes work precisely the opposite way. Taxes may be transferred from one individual to another, considering that there may be a shared obligation, as in the case of a group of individuals operating a business jointly. Sales tax is a tax imposed on sellers but frequently paid by them.

How Does Tax Work?

Taxes are levied on the general populace, whether individuals or corporate organizations, to raise money for the nation's welfare and infrastructure projects. Think of it this way: No citizen of a country has equal socioeconomic standing; thus, taxes from the wealthy are used to support the less fortunate through subventions on annual tax returns or other forms of financial aid.

Income taxes are imposed on a portion of a taxpayer's money. This money may include salary income, yields and returns from rising investment values, and dividends or interest earned as a secondary investment. The government then receives the tax money that was collected. Due to the extensive engagement of the government and regulatory agencies, I strongly advise my young readers to avoid any actions that may be considered tax evasion. Paying taxes on time is required since failing to do so might result in severe penalties.

You must understand how taxes function if you intend to work for someone, work for yourself, or someday own a business. The taxpayer will significantly depend on the type of tax and what regulations it comprises. For instance, the federal income tax in the United States only applies to individuals who earned a certain amount or had their gross income adjusted. Imagine that you are the owner of a company. Your firm would be formed to conduct business in a particular area or country; thus, your taxes would fall under the corporation tax category. It is crucial to remember that each tax is managed differently and may impose different requirements and exclusions on those who must pay the tax.

Everything takes time. It begins at the most basic level, and as you gain understanding, you can grasp more and more. If you start studying taxation, there will undoubtedly be a point when you can successfully maneuver the intricate tax systems and genuinely acknowledge that you are familiar with them. With knowledge, you would know the precise reporting and taxation obligations, the amounts that should be paid, and those that would be considered overpayments.

Your parents play a critical part in determining your financial destiny by teaching you the value of taxes and their role in everyone's life.

Moreover, as tax season approaches, education on valuable financial lessons and practices is *crucial*.

Taxation is a far broader issue than most young people tend to understand. Yet, you must embrace the concept because whether you know it or not, you are exposed to taxes from a young age but never contemplate them. For example, have you ever wondered why a product from a supermarket is so expensive, or more specifically, why it is more expensive once you get to the checkout?

In many cases, it is because of the sales tax. You will most likely learn about income tax when you land your first job, whether a white-collar one or a part-time position at a restaurant. Yet, such taxes and other kinds of taxes affect you from a very young age, starting from the first time you purchase something! You need to know this idea before you receive your first paycheck and discover deductions.

We need to consider the many forms of income that may be subject to taxation. Suppose you have a solid grasp of taxation from the outset of your adult life. In that case, you will undoubtedly know what taxes are, what you will pay, and what deductions you are entitled to. You will likely be able to plan throughout the year and manage your money correctly. Take the following advice: start filing your tax returns – or learn how to do so – as soon as you start earning money, whether you are working now or will in the future. You must submit taxes for the current tax year if your income surpasses $1,100 or if the sum of your pay plus an additional $350 exceeds that amount. No matter how much money you make, if your employer deducts taxes from your salary, you must submit a return to receive a refund.

Ask for Help!

If you need advice, don't hesitate to talk to your parents about becoming financially independent. Let's tackle the main point: it's always best to be honest about money matters.

The past few years have rocked the global economy, leading to financial challenges. It's normal for parents to want to protect you from stuff that might stress you out, but it's actually helpful for them to share the financial realities of your family with you.

Being open about not being able to buy something helps you see how money affects real life. Instead of zoning out during a long, boring lecture, ask your parents to break down money topics into short, easy-to-understand bits. Join them when they go to the bank, or watch them write a cheque so you can learn the basics of budgeting. Remember, you are the future leader who will take over when the adults are not around anymore. What you learn from your parents today will be passed down to future generations, keeping the tradition of financial security alive.

Understanding taxes is essential, so now we can discuss your expectations. Every little detail you learn will help you build a strong foundation in accounting and taxes, setting you up for success in your personal and professional life. Taxes can be complicated, covering property, payroll, and real estate tax. Before diving in, knowing what you're getting into is good. People have a long history of disliking the tax department, but it is still essential to learn about it. Tax accounting is based on the Tax Code, and it is all about figuring out how much tax you'll owe based on your income.

You might think, "I'm 19. Why should I care about the IRS?" Well, let me break it down for you. As you age, you will have different jobs, save money, invest, start a business, buy a house, and more. The recent economic collapse has led to higher taxes, but have you ever noticed that billionaires like Elon Musk, Jeff Bezos, and Warren Buffet don't seem to struggle with taxes? That's because they have a solid understanding of the tax code and have sought advice from experts who do. Being familiar with the classics is often seen as a sign of a well-rounded person. But knowing the classics and the tax code? Now that's the mark of someone with their financial future in check.

Tax literacy is super critical, not only because it can help you in your personal life but also because it can open up new opportunities for you. Learning about taxes is not a full-time job but a valuable skill. More than your job-specific skills are needed to determine your success in the professional world. As you advance in your career, you will be responsible for finances, PR, and marketing. Having a solid understanding of taxes now will make it easier for you to navigate these challenges in the future. Not only will this knowledge be helpful in the corporate world, but it can also help you if you decide to start your own business, no matter the size. Plus, being well-rounded and knowledgeable in different areas will make you a more confident and exciting person to talk to.

To be financially literate is an essential part of being aware and informed. Search online for resources like "Financial Education Made Easy" or "Teach Me Finances." You'll find many links, blogs, websites, and videos to help you learn. Make a plan, consult different books, and read the business section of your daily paper. Before you know it, you'll have a solid grasp on the subject and be better prepared to make smart financial moves.

Tax Mistakes to Avoid

Believe it or not, your tax decisions today can have long-lasting consequences, sometimes in your adult life. It's easy to think that you're too young to worry about taxes or that they're too complicated to understand. But listen: understanding your tax obligations early on is a crucial component of financial literacy and a topic too important to ignore.

Firstly, consider the value of filing a tax return, even if you earned very little in a year. Many teens forgo filing because their income falls below the taxable threshold. While you may not owe any federal income tax, you might miss out on a refund. Taxes are usually withheld from your paycheck, and if you've earned less than the standard deduction, you will likely get all that money back. This isn't a minor change; it can sometimes be a sizable sum. More importantly, filing your taxes when you are young starts building a tax history, which can be helpful down the line when applying for financial aid for college or loans.

The idea that the youth don't need to worry about taxes perpetuates the problematic notion of financial disengagement. From the moment you earn your first dollar, you are part of the economic ecosystem, and the tax responsibilities that come with it shouldn't be taken lightly. An early blunder: If you report only some of your income and leave out the income you may receive in cash or via online platforms, it will catch up with you. The IRS is more equipped than ever to trace unreported income in the digital finance age. The penalties for tax evasion, even unintentional, can be steep.

Speaking of penalties, they can also accrue for late filing. Be aware of the tax calendar.

The deadline for filing federal income tax returns is usually April 15th, and missing this date can result in late fees and interest accumulating on any unpaid tax liability.

Remember, the clock starts ticking not when you realize your mistake but when the error occurs. If you cannot file by the deadline, you can request an extension, but that has its rules and is not a free pass to delay indefinitely.

Another frequent stumbling block is not paying more attention to state taxes. While the federal tax return gets most of the attention, most states have income taxes, too, with their own forms, deductions, and credits. Not understanding your state tax obligations can result in another layer of complications and penalties.

One more aspect to be keenly aware of is the designation of dependents. If your parents claim you as a dependent on their tax return, there are limitations on what you can claim on your own return. Some teens mistakenly claim themselves, leading to a conflict that can cause delays and require amended returns. When it comes to taxes, communication with your parents is crucial.

Tax software and online platforms have made filing more effortless than ever, but you still need to understand it. These tools can handle straightforward tax situations well. Still, they might not capture the nuances applicable to you, particularly if you have multiple income sources or are eligible for specific credits or deductions. While hiring a tax professional might seem excessive for your seemingly simple financial life, a one-time consultation can offer invaluable insights and help you avoid costly mistakes.

The arena of taxes is fraught with complexities, and missteps can be both stressful and expensive. However, by engaging with your tax responsibilities early on, you gain invaluable experience and knowledge that will serve you well for the rest of your life. A proactive approach to understanding your taxes is a financial necessity and a rite of passage into informed adulthood. Don't let common mistakes deter you from taking that important step!

Making Financial Education Accessible to All

"Financial literacy is just as important in life as the other basics."[1]

John W. Rogers Jr., CEO of Ariel Capital Management

If I had to pick one extra subject that should be covered in school, it would be financial literacy. It's a skill lacking in many adults, not to mention teenagers, and that's not because of their failing; it simply isn't taught.

Think about why you picked up this book in the first place. Perhaps you were aware of how much you still had to learn about money; maybe you had big financial goals for the future and wanted to get ahead of the game. Whatever the reason, you needed to take matters into your own hands because you knew it wasn't information you were going to get in school.

Financial education is something we have to give ourselves. I wrote this book to empower you and others like you to take charge of that education, and I want it to be as accessible to as many young people as possible. For this reason, I've paused our journey for a moment: I'd like to ask you to get on board and help me disseminate this information.

I know you have a lot to think about already, and that probably sounds quite daunting, but it's surprisingly easy. All you need to do to help other young people find the information they need is write a short review online.

By leaving a review of this book on Amazon, you'll help other young people find all the guidance they need to take charge of their own financial education.

Reviews tell new readers a lot about a book and show them whether they've found what they're looking for. In just a few minutes, you can change the course of someone else's life. Isn't that incredible?

Thank you so much for your support. Now, let's get back on with our journey of money mastery!

Scan the QR code below to leave your review!

FIVE

Step 5: Budgeting: Living below your means

 "Success is no accident. It is hard work, perseverance, learning, studying, sacrifice and most of all, love of what you are doing or learning to do."

Pele

As you wise up with age and experience, you realize that all rules of success and achievement are universal and indivisible. They apply everywhere, and they apply to everything. Your financial well-being and stability are no exception. As a student, you must plan your budget prudence when your cash flow is low.

Organizing yourself will help you out in a big way. Remember that Mike Tyson declared bankruptcy in 2003. Allegedly, Floyd Mayweather, the prodigy believed to be a multi-millionaire, has been reported to owe millions in unpaid taxes to the IRS.

If you can't measure it, you can't manage it. There are multiple applications you can download right now to keep track of your cash inflow and outflow. [1]It is recommended that a teenager saves at least

20% of their money from a paycheck. Open a savings account and automatically transfer 1/5 of your money every time you get paid.

Create a blueprint chart for when your cash flow is low weekly, monthly, and year-end expenditures. Record every transaction you make. Did you go to Chipotle? Record that. Have you paid your phone bill? Record that. Have you got your weekly check? Record that. Track your income and your expenditures.

On top of that, separate the essential and non-essential spending. See what you spend the most on apart from your needs. Observe what comes up and see if you can reduce your spending. Tracking your monetary inflows and outflows will give you control over your funds.

Ask yourself: Where do you want to be in six months? In one year, five years, ten years?

Further along, set long-term and short-term goals. Short-term goals entail paying your semester fee and traveling to another state or country. Long-term goals entail your overall fiscal position. They project what assets you wish to have, what properties you want to own, and what portfolios you want. Your goals should be well within your reach.

Your goals should be realistic. They should align with where you stand and what you enjoy doing – don't set unrealistic goals, or you risk giving up on them altogether. [2]According to the Corporate Finance Institute, "SMART goals set you up for success by making goals specific, measurable, attainable, realistic, and timely. The SMART method helps push you further, gives you a sense of direction, and helps you organize and reach your goals".

Specific: The nuts and bolts of your Goal

Writing your goals down on paper helps to make them real and helps to keep you accountable. Be as detailed as possible about what you want to achieve, and organize it as short- and long-term goals. Some questions you want to ask yourself are:

- What do you want to accomplish?
- What do you need to do to achieve this specific goal?
- Are there any challenges that you have to overcome?

Measurable

This is an essential element of goal setting, which measures how long your goal will be accomplished. Organizing your short-term to long-term goals will be a good idea. You want to ask yourself:

- Is there a cost to help achieve this goal?
- When will this goal be accomplished?

Attainable: The strides to take to complete your Goal

In this stage of the goal-forming process, you want to use this to edit your goals. Putting in the time needed to reach your goals is essential, but you want to make this process manageable. If this becomes too much, ensure you re-evaluate and re-adjust as needed. The rule of thumb is to create smaller steps within the goal so that when you accomplish each step, it will motivate you to keep going.

Relevant

Having a laser-focused mindset, keeping your eye on the prize, and visualizing the outcome by setting some time each day will ensure you achieve your desired results.

Time

If you put a timeline out for each goal, this will help with your accountability to ensure you reach your goal by the set time. If you need extra time, you can continually re-adjust it as required, but always ensure that you include a timeline for completion. Leaving it open-ended risks goal abandonment, and we need to avoid this.

Make a plan to save money to pay at least a fraction of your college tuition. Or, make enough to help your parents with the bills. I don't expect you to be a millionaire by the end of this year, but at least you can save enough to do something substantial. Take one thing from me: money is all about mindset. **Approach money with a fresh and positive attitude; you will always have money and ideas to make it.**

Student Tips and Tricks

Now, consider a few student-specific tips and tricks. For example, always ask if there is a student discount. Many places offer student discounts, even online, that they don't necessarily promote. Likewise, you might find student specials, such as free admission on Tuesdays for Students to go to museums, etc.

Remember to consider how your parents can help you. You can discuss money with them and have them show you your mistakes so you can quickly correct them and learn from them. You can also use apps to input numbers to have a visual chart, which is easier to look at and understand, so you can track your money. You develop good money habits this way!

Years ago, I paid little attention to my spending habits and had a lot of credit card debt. I had to create a plan to fix it. I started using Quicken, the money-tracking software that tracks every transaction I make. It was hard at first, but it quickly became second nature.

Now, I know exactly where my money goes and can spot areas of excessive spending. Next, I added my monthly bills (mortgage, taxes, insurance, car loan, utilities, etc.). The total was $2400 per month. I get paid weekly, so I divided the amount by four, resulting in $600 per week (if you are paid biweekly, divide by 2 to get $1200).

Then, I opened three bank accounts: The main one, the chequing, and two separate savings accounts. My pay is directly deposited into the chequing account – $150 each to the savings accounts, and the rest remains in the main chequing account. If you can't split direct deposits, manually transfer the calculated amount each week. This ensures all my bills are covered when they are due, and I won't accidentally overspend. The money in the main chequing is for food, gas, and utility expenses. Using Quicken-like software helps me know my account balances at all times. The key is not spending more than what is in the primary chequing account.

Pay Back Your Credit!

If you use credit cards for cash back, charge what you have in the primary chequing and pay off the balance weekly. Transfer any leftover money to the savings account at the end of the week, or set a fixed amount to save weekly. The average number of weeks a month is 4.33, meaning you will get an extra paycheck four times a year. This additional money can be reserved or moved to your savings account.

Indeed, budgeting is a concept used across the spectrum from the smallest unit of society to the largest, i.e., from an individual to the state. Future planning is essential for survival. Let's draw another analogy to make it simple for you to understand. Think of a machine. Despite its tailored parts, measured down to millimeters, and strict quality controls, it requires something trivial to function smoothly: lubrication. A device needs to be oiled well for smooth functioning.

What makes a business run smoothly? It's cash. Cash Flow creates ease. The same applies to your personal life. Now, that money you are bringing in requires organization and targeted spending. Tax lawyers, accountants, auditors, and financial analysts are paid. These professionals are the ones you need on your team to help provide you with professional guidance for managing funds.

I have a short tale to narrate to you. This little story is native to South Asia. There was once a family: a husband, a wife, and their only son. The son was a young man in his mid-teens, old enough to help his father in the fields, cultivating crops. The boy, however, was reluctant to step out of the house. The concerned parents would be wrathful for the lazy boy for not working. After some time, the boy agreed to accompany his father to the field, but only to get away from his house and give a false impression that he was working. He wouldn't work. His father gave him a nickel before heading home so he could show it to his mother. When the boy showed the nickel to his mother, she instantly took it and threw it on the burning stove. The boy protested that she had thrown away his earnings. The mother stayed quiet. The day after, the same incident happened. The boy protested again.

The boy got his hands dirty on the third day and worked with his father. He earned an honest wage that day. Excited to tell his mother about his first pay, he rushed home. The mother again took the nickel and threw it on the burning stove. The boy immediately went after it and put his hand in the blazing fire. The boy protested intensely. The silent mother finally spoke. *"Today is the day you have earned it, my boy."* These habits, instilled now, will pay you throughout your career and life.

Now consider *spending*. If you have studied economics or plan to study it soon, you will know that spending is a way to ensure wealth growth. Although this is very accurate, there are levels and layers to it, nuances that you should understand before you go out and blow all your cash on partying. Simply said, don't spend the money you don't have.

Carefully thought out spending does not mean you have to spend only on your absolute needs. It would be best to pay for things that give you the most value. For example, spending $40 on a programming language course? Go ahead. Spending $40 on a jacket you don't need? Think twice. One more thing to remember: feel free to ask for what you are entitled to. For instance, many bookstores, clothing brands, and other outlets offer student discounts. When purchasing, either look for a place that already provides one or show up and ask for one. What is the worst that can happen? They will say no—no problem with that. These discounts are not only limited to shopping. They can be found almost everywhere. Want to go on an educational trip to a museum? Look for one that has prescribed days for students to roam around the history alleyways for free. Find festivals and competitions where students are encouraged to participate and sign up.

The discipline it requires might be daunting, and you might be afraid that you might fail. This thread leads to another concept, another skill you should master: self-accountability. A person who can keep himself in check and bridled to his values and rules can conquer any fear. Here is a question for you: are you responsible enough?

You may have noticed your parents using that one strategy you have always despised while shopping for basic necessities: asking for discounts and using coupons. Growing up, I used to step out of the shop or hide my face due to sheer disappointment and embarrassment, thinking about what others would think about us. But I was entirely incorrect! I have come to realize this while becoming a parent myself. Cutting prices and requesting discounts do not make you appear cheap; even if they did, you should not care.

Parents adopt this habit because they recognize money's necessity and significance. We, the older generation, know the importance of financial budgeting, and we can be sure that our parents adhere to it. I want you to embody this. Looking at them, do you notice your parents make a nice living? When you examine yourself, do you earn the same amount annually or monthly? The response could be a startling NO. Then, why do you still have a colossal ego every time you go to the grocery store with your parents if you don't get paid the same? Start concentrating on the things that are most important to you. Choose anything you believe will benefit your financial well-being, and implement those strategies immediately.

Asking for minor discounts is one tactic I focus on since they may add up to a sizable sum. This tactic goes a long way toward assisting you in successfully and efficiently managing your spending, especially when purchasing both pricey and inexpensive goods. With every cent you save, you first build a budgeting habit that will be beneficial in the long term, and second, you could have enough money to spend on something extremely essential. Asking for student discounts is good; trust me when I say that. You might only have enough money to cover your basic needs if you are a student. If you find a jacket or a pair of shoes you want to purchase, ask the retailer for a student discount. You might be surprised that they do offer discounts. If they don't, asserting yourself to ask while you have the opportunity does not hurt.

Few store owners are reluctant to give you a student discount; most store owners and shopkeepers know how vital student discounts are for young people trying to make ends meet. These adults you see now were once in your position and can appreciate it when someone asks for a student discount since they once shared it. This is how things have been going. Asking has never harmed anyone, but saving has always come on top.

Why is Budgeting important?

Budgeting and goal setting go hand-in-hand. Budgeting is what brings your objectives to life. A goal without budgeting will not work out how you want and can bring unnecessary stress and setbacks.

[3]A full 59% of parents said they financially helped an adult child in the past year, while 44% of adult children said they had received financial help from a parent in the same period.

Of those 44% of young adults, the majority (68%) were 18-to-24-years old. But 30% of adults between 30 and 34 also said they got financial assistance from a parent.

The poll is not to scare you but to bring home the reality of going into adulthood without developing a solid financial foundation. It is okay for a parent to help you out, but it is good practice to put a plan in place so that you can build a strong foundation. This can take a little time, but weave it into your goal-setting process.

Budgeting Techniques

Budgeting can benefit everyone of all ages mired in a web of complex financial commitments. It's a vital skill for anyone who earns, spends, or saves money—which includes you. Let us explore why budgeting is essential and the mistakes to avoid as you begin your journey toward financial independence.

This is your moment for discovery and exploration, including the realization that freedom is closely linked to economic stability. You may be earning money from a part-time job or an allowance, spending it on things that matter to you—clothing, gadgets, outings with friends—and possibly even saving a bit. But do you have a plan?

Most importantly, do you know where your money goes each month?

Start by understanding your income, including your allowance, any money earned from part-time work, and possibly even gifts on birthdays or holidays. Knowing what comes in is the first step in understanding what can reasonably go out. If you are working, remember to consider taxes, as this will reduce your take-home pay.

Recognize your expenses, which can be more complex than you might initially think. There are fixed costs, like monthly subscriptions to streaming services or phone bills, and variable expenses, such as meals out, shopping, or the occasional ticket to a concert or movie. Your costs may include school supplies, gas money if you drive, and, let's remember, seasonal prices like gifts for family and friends.

Here is where many people stumble: 'invisible expenses.' These small, often spontaneous purchases—a cup of coffee here, an online game add-on—may not seem significant but can quickly add up. Ignoring these minor expenses is a critical mistake because they often form a substantial part of your spending.

Now, how do you bring income and expenses together? The old-fashioned way is to note everything, make expense categories, and then compare them to your income. Nowadays, several apps can do this automatically for you, categorizing expenses and setting budgets for each type.

Now that everything is organized, what's next? Here is where strategic thinking comes in. If you find that your income is less than or just about equal to your expenses, it's time to reassess. Either find ways to increase your revenue—perhaps by taking extra shifts at work or launching a freelance project—or decrease your expenses.

Cutting costs does not mean giving up what you love. It just means finding more cost-effective alternatives.

Instead of buying coffee daily, why not invest in a good coffee maker? Love reading? A library card is a lot cheaper than buying books. Are you a fan of workouts? Many free resources can replace that expensive gym membership. The idea is not to stop living your life but to find a balance between what you want now and what you will need in the future.

Lastly, remember to consider the importance of setting financial goals, both short-term and long-term. Whether buying a new smartphone, saving for a car, or even starting a college fund. Proper planning gives your budget purpose and direction. They make the sacrifices worthwhile.

Pitfalls To Avoid When Budgeting

Setting and Forgetting Your Budget

Your life as a teenager is in flux—school demands, social commitments, and personal preferences change. Your budget needs to be flexible to accommodate this ever-changing landscape. Review it monthly or even weekly, and adjust as needed. Setting unrealistic goals can end up discouraging you.

Remember to set smaller goals within your main goal so that each mini-goal you reach will give you the incentive and drive to carry on.

Too Strict

If your dreams feel like you are wearing a straitjacket at times, then this is a sign that your goals need to be re-adjusted to be less rigid so that you enjoy the process along the way and to keep you motivated. Ensure your budget leaves room for rising costs of items and for a bit of leeway for extra spending.

Impulse Purchasing

When you go shopping with your friends, I know that you may see something you must have, but remember that if you see something, don't buy it on the spot. Instead, go home and give it a couple of days to think about it. If you evaluate and decide to have this item, calculate to ensure you have the funds for it and buy it, and determine how much this will be a setback and delay in accomplishing your primary goal. You may want to think about creating a small budget for impulse purchases so that you can have room to buy things on a whim.

Not Saving Your Money

Keep an emergency fund. I know it sounds terribly adult, but unexpected expenses are not age-specific. They can happen to anyone, including you. Whether replacing a lost phone or facing sudden medical costs, an emergency fund provides a financial cushion that can be a lifesaver.

The Importance of a Support Group

On that note, I would like to outline the importance of surrounding yourself with "Cheerleaders" or other people who are also open to budgeting and organizing finances. A good group of like-minded friends and your parents will support and encourage you to keep going on your path to budgeting.

Budgeting is not just about restricting spending but empowering you to live on your terms. A budget is not a set of limitations; it's a set of possibilities. It teaches you the value of money, the importance of discipline, and the satisfaction of attaining goals you set for yourself. More importantly, it sets the stage for your financial future, teaching you lessons many adults learn too late. It is better to learn from the older generation's mistakes, see the repercussions of not having a financial plan, and use that as a firm reminder to avoid that pitfall and waste years of learning the lesson the hard way.

So, take the first step. Sit down, take a deep breath, and create your first budget. Mistakes will be made, but that's part of the learning curve. What matters is the habit, the mindset, and the financial awareness you build today, which will serve you well for the rest of your life.

SIX

Step 6: Make More Money, Repeat!

 "An investment in knowledge pays the best interest."

Benjamin Franklin

Investing may seem overwhelming, but it does not have to be complicated.

Have an objective. What exactly are you striving for if an aim is not in sight? Take a marathon runner as an example. The runner follows the lines to get to the finish line, correct? He has a target and a reward for aspiring. He may simply go around in circles all day long without achieving his goals if there is no clear winner or no specific purpose to do it.

It is best to use good judgment and to have aspirational goals. Investing is what will bring you to your financial goals faster. Establish a plan for successfully achieving those objectives and earning the reward. Consider someone who consistently works out and forgoes cheat meals throughout the week to store extra calories for just one cheat meal during the entire week to help make things simpler for them. With that cheat day in mind, they may put in the ideal amount of work and effort needed to achieve and enjoy a satisfying cheat meal.

Invest in Yourself

Investing in yourself can be a great way to boost your earnings, especially if you're looking for ways to grow your money quickly. But what exactly does "invest in yourself" mean? It's all about spending money and time learning new skills that can help you earn more.

For instance, you could buy a toolkit and take an affordable course to learn how to use the tools effectively. The important thing is that you start. There is no better way than to use that money to learn and then take action to develop that skill. Some adults might have the money but need more time and energy. Teenagers often have the time and energy but need the funds. Why not take on tasks like shoveling snow from driveways or cleaning swimming pools to make extra cash in the short term? Ultimately, it's up to you what you do with your money. Consider saving some of it in a savings account to help secure your financial future.

That being said, long-term investments might be the way to go if you want to invest your money for long-term growth rather than a quick increase. With these investments, there might be times when you wish to withdraw your funds but have yet to see the results you hoped for. Long-term investments can be a good option for young people who want to put their money to work without constantly worrying about it. Plus, they can help curb impulsive spending habits that some teenagers struggle with. This will, in turn, boost your income and diversify your investments; it is essential to learn about the financial system.

This includes financial markets and institutions that handle everything money-related, like lending, borrowing, and investing funds. Banks are the most well-known financial institutions, primarily providing loans to individuals and businesses while charging interest to make a profit. They also offer other services that could increase your earnings, such as various account types that provide returns over time.

Institutions offer financial services like mutual funds, hedge funds, insurance companies, pension funds, brokerage houses, and index funds. By expanding your knowledge of these institutions and their services, you will be better equipped to make intelligent financial decisions and grow your wealth long-term.

Get a Coach

Having a coach is an invaluable tool that will guide you toward self-improvement and help you achieve your goals quickly. A coach is a game-changer in turning discouragement into encouragement by assisting you in developing a plan to get and stay organized by managing a schedule that will allow you to alleviate stress and guide you to keep your eye on the prize. The best athletes have coaches. Everyone from all ages and stages of life can benefit from a coach. You can hire a coach by asking your guidance counselor for recommendations or check out www.coachbit.com.

Investment Opportunities

The importance of setting yourself up financially from a young age cannot be overstated. You might think investing is strictly the domain of the middle-aged, the buttoned-up, or the economically savvy, but there is always a right time to start young, especially when meeting short-term goals. Surprisingly, these short-term aims can set the foundation for your financial future. Firstly, let's cut through the jargon. At its core, investing means investing your money into assets that can grow over time. These assets can range from stocks and bonds to real estate and start-ups. But setting clear goals is essential before you plunge headfirst into the stock market or any other type of investment. What are you investing for? A new laptop? A car? College?

Once you have a goal, you can estimate how much money you will need and when you will need it. For short-term goals—those you hope to achieve in less than three years—you will likely want safer, more stable investments. You won't make a fortune overnight, but you won't risk losing much of your money. Look into Certificates of Deposit (CDs) or high-yield savings accounts, which offer relatively modest but secure returns. Even a good old-fashioned piggy bank can be an excellent short-term investment vehicle if disciplined about feeding it regularly.

Budgeting goes hand in hand with investing. Knowing how much you earn, how much you spend, and how much you can comfortably invest is essential. Consider setting automatic savings with your bank so that you can determine the amount from your earnings that will automatically go to your savings account on payday. You need to set this up once, and as your pay increases, you can increase the amount that the bank will automatically take out to add to your savings.

Exchange-Traded Funds

Exchange-Traded Funds (ETFs) are Index-based and considered less risky investments. ETFs represent a large group of companies, allowing you to invest in many stocks simultaneously. When considering stocks or ETFs for short-term goals, do your homework to research companies, watch market trends, and practice with some virtual stock trading apps before putting real money on the line. Check out the stock market index that measures stock performance: S&P 500, NASDAQ, Dow Jones Industrial Average. When researching the companies you want to buy stocks from, you can check out websites like Yahoo! Finance, Market Watch.com, and stock analysis.com.

Every investment decision provides you with invaluable experience. You learn to analyze risks, read market trends, and cope with the financial market's inevitable ups and downs. These lessons lay the groundwork for the more complex investment strategies you may adopt as an adult, looking towards long-term goals like retirement or purchasing a home. Remember, while focusing on short-term gains, you are gaining long-term wisdom.

Some might think, "But I don't have much money!" That's entirely okay. You don't need thousands of dollars to begin investing. Many online platforms enable you to start with as little as $5. The key is to make investing a habit. Regular, disciplined contributions, even a tiny amount, can grow significantly over time due to the magic of compound interest.

A crucial aspect often overlooked by young investors is the cost of investing. Be aware of the fees associated with your investment options. High fees can eat into your returns and make it much harder to reach your goals. Always read the fine print and opt for low-fee or no-fee options whenever possible.

Let's remember taxes. Though it may sound far-fetched now, certain types of income from investments are taxable. For instance, if you are dabbling in the stock market, you must report any gains when tax time rolls around.

Whether your goal is to buy a new smartphone, pay for a summer trip, or simply build a rainy-day fund, smart investing can help you achieve it. It's not just about the short-term returns; it's about setting yourself up for a lifetime of financial freedom. With research, discipline, and foresight, you can achieve your short-term goals and set the foundation for your long-term financial health.

After all, the best time to start investing is not in your 30s, 40s, or 50s; the time is now.

Your Financial Journey

Let us examine some options you can explore to set up your portfolio and begin your financial journey.

The daily banking transactions are generous. Some banks allow up to a $100 limit on bank transactions and up to $500 on the debit card. Keep in mind that you have other options. There are several different platforms you can explore.

High-Yield Savings Account

These accounts offer high-interest rates for your deposits. You can put your pocket money in them, or your parents or grandparents can make deposits for you. You may wonder if we have already discussed saving accounts, so why not deposit money in them? A regular savings account does not pay the interest of a high-yield savings account. Hence, the name 'high-yield.' These accounts are risk-free and insured up to $250,000 by the Federal Deposit Insurance Corporation. [1]FDIC insurance covers chequing, savings, and other deposit accounts up to a standard amount of $250,000 — but there are a few caveats. Namely, the $250,000 limit is per account holder, not per account, as you might think.

Certificates of Deposit

Then come the certificates of deposit (CD). CDs are another product of the banks that allow you to put your savings in them and earn interest in return. There is a catch. The condition for signing up for this account is that your money has to be kept there for a specific number of months, even years. At maturity, you can acquire your principal amount and the interest you earned over the months and years. This is an excellent way to save up for something big and memorable. It could be your college fee, a start-up, or for your dream car.

Similar products offered by banks are stocks and bonds. Bonds are issued to individuals who lend money to a company or a government entity. In return, you earn interest over your loaned-out amount. Stocks, or shares, give you ownership of a company. Against your purchase of stocks, you receive dividends, i.e., profits from the company's business.

Although the options seem limitless, there are specific platforms where you will be subject to a "custodial account." A custodial account is where your parents or legal guardian opens an account for you. The purpose is to prepare you to act independently and save for future expenses.

The Unsung Hero: Diversification in Investments

Have you ever heard the phrase, "Don't put all your eggs in one basket"? It's an old adage but exceptionally relevant to investing.

Simply put, diversification is about spreading your investments across asset classes like stocks, bonds, and real estate. No investment is foolproof; each comes with its unique set of risks. By diversifying, you are not betting your entire financial future on a single turn of the wheel. This practice doesn't guarantee against losses, but it reduces the impact any poor-performing investment could have on your overall portfolio.

If you are from Canada, your parents probably opened an RESP account on your behalf as a baby. This account is designed to help you save for your education. You can choose different investment vehicles to grow your RESP, such as stocks, bonds, mutual funds, and GICs. GICs are Guaranteed Investment Certificates. The interest rates are not high, but it is considered one of the safest investments because your initial investment is protected.

Consider opening up a 401(k) Retirement Plan. People usually set them up at the beginning of their careers to ensure a safe and profitable retirement. But that's neither a compulsion nor a condition. If you are 18, you are good to go; just check with state laws.

Compounding

Now, let's switch over to a different aspect of investing: compounding. Compounding is a process by which earnings on an asset are reinvested and credited to the existing principal. You may also understand it by the term "the snowball effect." It keeps expanding in size as it continues to roll downhill. That's a funny analogy because compounding shall only take your earnings uphill!

I understand that many concepts and theories in finance can seem daunting, but if there is one concept you must understand fully, it is compounding.

An example will help you understand more easily.

Let's look at an example. Suppose $5,000 is deposited into a savings account at an annual interest rate of 5%, compounded monthly. In that case, the value of the investment after ten years can be calculated as follows.

P(Principal) = 5000: r (Interest Rate) = 5/100 = 0.05
n (Compounding Time) = 12
t (Time of maturity) = 10
If we apply the compounding formula
$$A = P(1 + r/n)^{(n*t)}$$
We arrive at the amount of: = 8235.05.
The total after ten years will be $8,235.05.

A deposit can be compounded monthly, bi-annually, or even yearly. Do you want the secret sauce to earn exponential amounts of money? Compounding is the answer. Check out www.thecalculatorsite.com and type in compound interest in the search bar for more details.

There is a catch. It takes time to compound. At this juncture, you should play the game wisely and play the long game. Why? Earnings are not strict; employing sustainable systems to make money is a skill few can master.

After laying out and delineating different options you can exploit, I recommend you do some research on your part.

Look up the websites of your local banks, or visit them and ask about what they can offer you. Keep exploring opportunities to secure your future. I know you want to become a millionaire, live in a mansion, and have an exotic car collection. There is a saying in Chinese: A journey of a thousand miles begins with a single step. Take the actions we have talked about and slowly take pace. You will get there one day.

The beautiful thing about money is that once you have enough, you no longer have to hustle to make more of it. Money creates money.

Gain money confidently, and watch it do wonders for you. Growing up where I am today, I have seen people your age work hard and achieve success. Making mistakes is part of the process, but it does not mean you give up. It just means you need to re-evaluate and change your strategy. Learning from books like this helps minimize mistakes made, as you learn from the wisdom of others and other people's mistakes. When money comes in, it is easy to spend on unnecessary things, but remember to keep your eye on the prize.

 " You will either learn to manage money, or the lack of it will manage you."

Dave Ramsey

Pay attention to the hustle, practice discipline, and see how you develop!

Compounding Made Easy

If you do not understand compounding yet, do not worry – I will explain it in more detail here. Compound interest may sound like a topic reserved for finance geeks and Warren Buffett, but understanding this concept early on can be your secret weapon to achieving financial freedom. If you have ever dreamed of buying a car, traveling the world, or becoming financially independent, compound interest should be your go-to strategy. And no, you don't have to be a Wall Street whiz kid to get it.

At its most basic, compound interest is the interest you earn on the initial amount of money you've saved or invested (the principal) and any interest you've already earned. It's interest *on* interest. While that might sound like a trivial difference compared to simple interest—which only earns you money on your initial deposit—it's anything but. Compound interest has a snowball effect. The larger the snowball gets, the faster it grows.

Have a look at this example. Say you start with $100 and earn an annual interest rate of 5%. In the first year, you would earn $5 in interest, bringing your total to $105. But in the second year, you are earning interest not just on your initial $100 but also on the new total of $105. So, you would earn $5.25 in the second year, not just another $5. That additional quarter might not sound like much, but it's a game-changer over the long term.

To clarify, I will use the following example: Let us consider two friends, Alex and Jamie, to highlight how impactful compound interest can be. Alex starts investing $200 a month at age 18 and continues doing so until age 28, then stops adding new money. That's 10 years of saving. On the other hand, Jamie doesn't start until he's 28 but continues to add $200 every month until he turns 58. Both earn an annual return of 7%.

At age 58, Alex would have around $402,000 even though he stopped contributing at age 28. Jamie, who saved for 30 years, would have around $372,000. Notice that? Alex invested for a shorter period but ended up with more money. That's compound interest at work.

The magic of compound interest is in its long-term power, so starting as early as possible is vital. We often hear about 'starting young,' but the concept comes to life when applied to compound interest. Time is your biggest ally. Even small sums can turn into fortunes if you are patient enough.

But it's not just about the money you could earn; it's also about the money you could owe. Compound interest can work against you through credit card debt, student loans, or any other borrowed money that accrues interest. Suppose you have a $1,000 credit card balance at an interest rate of 18%. If you only make the minimum payment and don't add any more charges to the card, it will take you 113 months (almost 10 years!) to pay it off, costing you about $923 in interest.

Compound interest can be maximized if you follow these fundamental principles, which must be kept in mind. Firstly, reinvest the interest you earn. It's tempting to cash out when you see extra money accumulating, but you will significantly boost your returns by letting it compound.

Be consistent. Thanks to compound interest, regular contributions can be amplified over the long term. Like a gym routine, the hardest part is sticking with it, but the results are well worth it.

Minimize withdrawals. When you take money out of your savings or investment account, you are not just losing that amount but also all the interest that money could have earned for years to come.

So whether you are saving up for something immediate, like a new gaming system, or something far in the future, like a home or retirement, understanding the power of compound interest is a critical skill. It's not just a formula or a line on a bank statement; it is a cornerstone of a competent financial strategy. The beauty of compound interest is that it requires no special skills, no insider tips, and no get-rich-quick schemes. It takes some initial effort, discipline, and patience to let your money grow over time.

In a world of instant gratification, compound interest's slow and steady nature might not seem appealing. But as you navigate life's financial maze, from paying for college to buying your first car and eventually preparing for a financially secure life, the enduring power of compound interest can serve as your North Star. It's more than math; it's your financial superpower waiting to be unleashed.

SEVEN

Step 7: The Savvy Teen - Side Hustles

 "Success is not final; Failure is not fatal: It is the courage to continue that counts."

Winston S. Churchill

Over the last few years, hustle culture has prevailed a lot. People slowly realize that their day job alone won't give them much. Therefore, they find something they can do part-time to make extra money and generate a small income stream. Many skilled professionals have now turned to freelance to make some extra cash. The existence of platforms exclusively built for this purpose has given rise to side hustles such as freelancing.

"Hustling": What Does it Mean?

The word hustle comes from the Dutch word "husselen," meaning "to hurry" or "busy." The connotation implies making money through illegal means, fraud, or deception. Some hustlers make money on the street, whereas others make money in marbled offices. The word hustle and its implications have recently changed their meaning. The "Hustle" is for honest people who want to make extra cash and pay the bills. However, the element of speed is still intact.

When you struggle to find jobs or work odd jobs, starting a side hustle might be your best decision. Don't think being young puts you at a disadvantage; this is the most significant advantage at your disposal. You have time and energy to experiment and determine what works best for you.

A side hustle can cover many costs for you. For instance, if you work at McDonald's, your net pay needs to be increased. A side hustle can be a quick and viable fix.

Starting a side hustle ensures one thing that even a regular job doesn't provide: consistent cash flow. You can only earn extra money through bonuses or commissions at your day job. We all know that rewards are not just handed to you. One has to work for months or even years to get a promotion. Consistent cash flow is essential!

Imagine an empty cup sitting under a tap. The tap constantly drips. Drop by drop, and the cup starts to fill up. Even if you drink the water, the faucet continues to drip. Another empty cup sits under a tap, but the difference is that this tap lets out a fast water flow, and then it closes. Afterward, no water comes out of that faucet for a long time. The next thing you know, the cup is as dry as the Sahara Desert. That is your monthly wage.

There are multiple utilities that side hustles have to offer. Relying on one source of income is tricky enough, and depending on one source of income that can be stopped at any moment is even more problematic. Financial security is as important as anything else you want to secure. Even if it is $50 a month, it is $50 more than you previously had. Another notable feature of a side hustle is the amount of control you can exert on it. In a 9-5 job, your life is in the hands of your supervisor or manager.

On the other hand, it's just you, a one-person army, in a side hustle. Your control over your side income allows you to be creative when needed. You also get to choose what you do, how, and with whom you want to do it.

Side Hustles Can Be Long-Term!

Keep in mind that a side hustle doesn't have to be short-lived. If you plan wisely, it can be long-term. There are many stories of people starting side hustles, either for fun or out of necessity, and later converting them into full-time, high-earning businesses. People have made dramatic career changes simply because their side hustle paid way more than their day job.

Be constantly on the lookout for ideas. Side hustles also provide you with an opportunity to explore yourself. You may try selling and realize that sales are something you want to do and you are good at. If you start a website designing gig, you may discover that your abilities are best suited for web designing. Also, these small ventures and gigs give you tremendous confidence and build on your skill set while adding value. Your confidence level will go through the roof as you grow in your career and start taking on more complex assignments and projects; while doing something independently, you gain experience and become savvy about the market.

It is a competitive advantage you will have over others. If you plan to do your own full-time business later on, the experience you will have from your younger years will put you on a higher pedestal. Early exposure to adverse conditions and inconvenient routines will toughen you up. If you survive this phase, which I'm sure you will, you can go anywhere, do anything, and leave your mark. Starting a hustle sounds fancy and cool, but staying consistent takes a lot of work. While it's true that side hustles should take only some of your time, it is also true that when you start, you will have to put in the work.

You must be thinking: can I make it with hustling? Absolutely!

If you are into hustling or have seen any content about financial freedom online, you must have come across Gary Vaynerchuk, commonly known as Gary Vee.

Gary Vee is the son of immigrant parents who left the Soviet Union for America. Right from the get-go, Gary Vee was a high-strung individual. He kept his eyes open for opportunities, even as a young kid. He dived into several things before becoming rich and famous. He is mainly known for yard sales. He used to show up to a yard sale, buy old baseball cards, mugs, sports T-shirts, etc., and flip them to make a profit. That is just one of his many endeavors, and all were done while he was young. He is often heard saying that if there's one thing he would go back in time for, it would be to be young again.

When you are young, you move differently. You have the most energy. If you hear Gary Vee talk, you will find him excited and flared up. You might think that now he is a millionaire, why doesn't he retire peacefully? And why does he even talk like that? What's the rush? It would be best to realize that this discipline, commitment, focus, and motivation got him there. All he did was take the first step. He used all this hustle-I.Q. to run his parents' wine business. He increased the business's profits from $3 million to $60 million. The work ethic he instilled in himself resulted from his work as a young boy. The same pathway is open for you as well. To build a side business and make your dreams real.

Figuring out why you want to start a side hustle is crucial. Are you working to party with your friends, to increase your income, boost your emergency savings, or to have the ability to invest the extra money you make? Is this to fulfill your short-term or long-term goals? Mindset is crucial. You must first pinpoint the primary motivator for establishing a side business. You will understand how to handle your day-to-day issues and will be able to create and run the same side gigs as you begin to understand why you came up with them. You'll remain focused and become more goal-oriented this way!

Being honest about your skills and interests is essential when looking for a side gig. Imagine wanting to sell cars as a side business, but this is the first time you've sold something. Exploring opportunities in areas you are already familiar with is best to make your life easier. There is no need to take on extra work learning a new field when you can build on your existing strengths. To find the perfect side gig, you need the right mindset and enthusiasm for what you are doing. Remember, no website or person can find the ideal side job for you – it is up to you to research and decide. If things don't work out, it's better to know you made the choice rather than blame someone else.

Once you have chosen a side gig, start small and see where it takes you. Consistency and patience are crucial to success. By starting small, you are more likely to learn from your mistakes and make better investment decisions. For example, spending thousands on building a website without customers would not make sense. That money could be used for something more beneficial.

Time management is crucial when balancing a side gig with your daily responsibilities. It might seem easy initially, but juggling work, school, and a side business can be challenging. Create a daily routine that benefits your primary responsibilities and side gig to avoid burnout. These essential tips can help you find success in your side gig journey. Remember to start small, prioritize your time, and choose something that aligns with your skills and interests. It might seem confusing at first, but exploring the world of side gigs can be an exciting and rewarding experience.

Finding a Side Hustle

So, where do you start? The digital age has democratized the way we can make money. Websites like Etsy, eBay, and Depop allow you to sell handmade crafts, vintage clothes, or even digital art. Social media channels can be monetized through sponsored posts if you have a sizable following. If you are tech-savvy, consider freelancing in graphic design or web development. Platforms like Fiverr and Upwork can connect you with clients needing various services. Are you good at a particular school subject? Turn that expertise into a tutoring service. The possibilities are endless, limited only by your imagination and willingness to hustle.

Now, as you venture into the world of side hustles, there are a few considerations to remember.

Firstly, be realistic about your time commitments. School, homework, and extra-curricular activities are still priorities; a side hustle should maintain these.

Secondly, consider the costs. Whether it's the price of materials for your Etsy shop or the subscription fee for a website, understand the initial and ongoing expenses. Keep track of these costs meticulously. This habit doesn't just help you understand your profitability; it also introduces you to the critical business skill of accounting.

Thirdly, understand your target market. Who are you selling to? What are they willing to pay? This requires market research; getting it right means you can use your time and resources effectively.

Perhaps the most overlooked aspect of a side hustle is its educational value. Beyond the skills you gain, you are also learning how to market your services, deal with clients, and manage your finances. These are life skills that many adults wish they had learned earlier.

Lastly, consider the legal aspects. Even as a teen, you'll likely need to report your earnings when tax season rolls around. While it may be a tedious process, it is also a Practical lesson in adulting. Keep records of your income and any business-related expenses. Apps and software like QuickBooks or Mint can be beneficial for this.

Despite its challenges, the rewards of a side hustle extend beyond the financial. It can bring a sense of independence and valuable skills to serve you well into adulthood. Not to mention, it can also be a lot of fun. After all, you are making money doing something you love, setting your hours, and calling the shots.

The world is changing, and conventional paths to financial security are no longer as reliable as they once were. Side hustles offer an alternative route to diversify your skills and income streams. For young people standing on the precipice of adulthood, stepping into the world of side hustles can offer a more immediate form of financial independence and a toolkit of skills you will carry with you for life.

Succeeding in Your Side Hustle

What does it take to succeed? Let's have a look.

Recognize Your Skillset

The first step is introspection. Questions to ask yourself are: what are you good at? What do you enjoy doing? How can I solve a common problem that people can benefit from my services?

Recognizing your skill set and aligning it with market demand is crucial. If you are a computer whiz, remote IT consulting might be your alley. Platforms like Fiverr or Upwork offer a great starting point if you have a knack for graphic design. Passion fuels perseverance, and you will need many of the latter to make your side hustle successful.

Start Small

Many successful entrepreneurs did not start with grand plans; they started small and scaled up. You should, too. Test the waters with a minimal investment of time and resources. Use this phase to gauge demand, identify potential pitfalls, and understand what you are getting into. This is your learning curve, so make the most of it.

Maintain Balance

I know that you have other responsibilities, including school, extracurricular activities, family obligations, and a part-time job. Your side hustle should complement, not interfere with, these responsibilities. Time management is crucial here. Develop a realistic timetable that allocates hours to your side hustle without neglecting your other commitments.

Market Yourself

To master the art of marketing in a world where attention spans are much shorter, standing out is ever more essential in a world where everyone vies for attention.

Research what is in demand, and use winning marketing strategies to ensure people know what you offer through social media marketing or word-of-mouth. Consider creating a portfolio or a small website that showcases your work. Create an Instagram account for your side business and collaborate with influencers for a nice exposure boost.

Be honest and share real stories. This allows people to see who you are and create a connection with you. If they can relate to your story, they will know your value and want to benefit from it. By doing this, you will notice that they will begin to seek you out.

Ensure that you stay trendy and current. Always aim to keep learning as market trends shift, consumer needs evolve, and new tools and technologies emerge.

Staying abreast of these changes keeps your side hustle relevant and elevates your expertise. Subscribe to newsletters and consider taking short courses to upgrade your skills.

You can use youth to your advantage because teenagers are generally excited, curious, and open to new ideas. With this information, research your niche and focus on how to keep your audience interested. Use your networks, both online and offline, to spread the word.

The Nuts and Bolts

A side hustle is not just about making money; it's also about managing it. Know your operating costs, set realistic pricing, and meticulously track your income and expenses. These financial habits determine the viability of your side hustle and teach you valuable financial management lessons. Suppose you have taken action after reading each chapter in this book and have created your budget chart to manage your income and expenses. In that case, you may have noticed that you are easing into the excellent habit of tracking your expenses. From your chart, you can see what your budget allows for your side hustle. You can also create a small column in your chart to add the potential income you expect to receive from your side hustle and use that as your target goal for extra profit.

Legal and Tax Considerations

Considering a side hustle's legal and tax aspects is crucial. Research your local laws about running a small business. Understand how to report your income during tax season and keep meticulous records of all your financial transactions.

Success in a side hustle doesn't happen overnight or by accident. It culminates in hard work, effective planning, and continuous learning.

The benefits, however, go beyond the monetary. A successful side hustle equips you with a diversified skill set, teaches you the nuances of running a business, and fosters a sense of independence and confidence that will serve you well in your journey toward adulthood.

So, venture out and test your entrepreneurial waters. Through calculated steps, balanced commitments, and a continuous learning approach, your side hustle could become more than just an extra source of income—it could be the stepping stone to your future.

Plan for the Long Haul

While your immediate goal might be to make some extra cash, consider what this will look like in the long term. Could your side hustle become a full-time job? Or is it a stepping stone to a career path you are passionate about? A forward-thinking approach can turn a small venture into a significant part of your life's journey.

EIGHT

Step 8: Time Management

> *"Productivity is never an accident. It is always the result of a commitment to excellence, intelligent planning, and focused effort."*
>
> Paul J. Meyer

Trying to manage work and school may sometimes become psychologically and physically draining. However, working while enrolled in high school, college, or university might be advantageous for various reasons. The most important thing is balancing work and study since, if done well, it will become manageable.

The state of the global economy has made things challenging for students like you, and the rising cost of education often pushes many to seek part-time jobs to cover expenses and maintain financial stability. We understand that you face unique challenges at this stage of your life, and we have immense respect for your resilience. With increasing pressure, unexpected situations can arise, and some teens may even consider leaving school.

Why do some teenagers think about dropping out? It might be because they need help to balance a demanding schedule and a heavy workload. It's natural to feel overwhelmed, but things can become more manageable over time. If the thought of quitting still lingers, it might be a sign to reevaluate your motivation and goals.

Striking the Balance

Creating a healthy balance between school and work is possible. Though it might not be a perfect fit initially, why not try? With dedication and perseverance, you can make it work. Remember, it's a learning experience that will take time, and this chapter of your life can be an excellent opportunity to gain valuable knowledge without compromising your education. Time management is the key! Prioritizing your time and being effective is essential for establishing a successful balance between school and work. Embrace time management as your secret weapon for thriving during this exciting and challenging phase of your life.

 "Time isn't the main thing, it's the only thing."

— Miles Davis

Balancing work and studies can be difficult, but it's important to remember that with the right approach, you can manage both. Time management is vital here.

Try to find a part-time job that offers flexible hours. This will allow you to plan your time, set priorities, and make room for academics and leisure activities.

Remember that you can't do everything. Prioritize your essential tasks and plan your day to meet deadlines and exam dates. Recognizing the importance of prioritizing can help you avoid last-minute stress.

It's unrealistic to expect yourself to work 16-17 hours a day while only getting 5-6 hours of sleep, even with good time management. While it's essential to maintain a healthy balance between work, life, and school, there will be challenges. Your sleep might be affected, which can have negative consequences.

Finding a healthy balance can help you grow personally, professionally, and academically, allowing you to apply effective time management strategies. Allocate an appropriate amount of time for sleep, and you will find that life becomes more manageable. You will be more focused in class, retain more information, and be more efficient in completing tasks, which will help you meet your academic and work commitments.

Be honest about how much time and energy you can devote daily. For example, some part-time jobs may be busier during certain months, which might conflict with your exam schedule. Consider how much time you'll need to manage everything effectively. Be aware that some employers might take advantage of eager students who want to start earning money, so carefully plan your schedule to avoid potential issues in the future.

 "All time management begins with planning."

Tom Greening

As someone who has been in your shoes, I understand your challenges. Taking on part-time work while managing your studies might seem overwhelming. Still, you can balance your academic and professional life with a well-planned schedule and effective time management. This approach can help reduce procrastination and boost productivity.

Ask yourself, are you working intelligent or just working hard? Hard work is essential, but sometimes, finding a more innovative way to achieve a goal can save you time and effort. Prioritizing clever work over sheer hard work can make a difference in managing your time.

Lessons from the Swiss

One thing to admire about the Swiss is their focus on time management and organization, which started when they were young. Swiss clocks are famous worldwide because they understand the value of time.

You may be familiar with the saying "Time is money," which resonates across cultures and emphasizes the importance of time management for success. Maximize your time, maintain a healthy balance, and prepare for unexpected events. Prioritize what's most essential and give it your all. Growing up in a household where I needed to succeed and secure a stable financial future, this advice helped me get to where I am today. Remember, prioritizing and focusing on what truly matters can make a significant difference in your life.

Maintaining a healthy balance and time management is crucial for maximizing your years. If you still need to focus on these aspects, now is the time to start. The key is prioritizing tasks that help you reach your goals more quickly. By doing this, you can balance important work and other aspects of your life. Your young years are full of energy and potential—you might feel like you can conquer the world. Having that enthusiasm is great, but remember not to get swept away by the excitement. Money is essential, but so is maintaining perspective on your broader goals.

When starting a part-time job, feeling excited or anxious is normal. Earning your first money, no matter the amount, can be a confidence booster. But remember that part-time jobs are meant to complement your bigger goals, not consume all your time and energy. Work hard and be committed, but remember to leave room for other aspects of your life. In fact, being a well-rounded individual means finding a balance between your family, friends, education, and work. Refrain from letting your pursuit of financial freedom take precedence over your social, academic, and family life. Strive to create harmony among all these areas to make the most of your youth.

Work-life balance is something that only some achieve. It is the core principle, a secret, a mirage that even the most successful CEOs and business magnates seek. One of the fundamental reasons they fail to make time for family and leisure is this: When they worked from the ground up, the seeds they sowed were strictly meant to grow their wealth, not to cultivate values. Yes, money can, and it definitely does make you happy. But all this cash and no time? Savvy people in business pay money to buy time, and the not-so-smart ones give time to make money. It would be best if you learned from it. Plan out a schedule and make appointments if you have to, but give time to your studies, family, friends, and most importantly, yourself. I highly recommend using the Pomodoro Technique. This genius idea was created by Francesco Cirillo while he was in school in the late 1980s to help manage his time effectively to get tasks done. [1]Cirillo went on to write a book about his method; its biggest strength is its simplicity:

1. Get a to-do list and a timer.
2. Set your timer for 25 minutes, and focus on a single task until the timer rings.
3. When your session ends, mark off one Pomodoro and record what you completed.
4. Then, enjoy a five-minute break.
5. After four Pomodoros, take a longer, more restorative 15-30 minute break.

This is a great way to measure time management. If you need more time for a more significant project, you can break it up into smaller bits to create minor completion within the big project so that it can get done promptly.

A side hustle is something different from a part-time job. With the influence of the internet and "hustle culture," it might seem like you should be working 18 hours a day, but that's not necessarily the case. A side hustle is a part-time gig that brings in extra cash with minimal effort and time. It can even serve as a pilot project for a potential start-up if that's your goal. But if you're juggling a part-time job and a side hustle, be careful to manage your time wisely so they don't interfere with each other. Sticking to a schedule is essential.

We will also discuss balancing your social life, like hanging out with friends.

People are social creatures, and spending time with friends and loved ones can be a great way to relieve stress and find inspiration. Instead of bragging about how much money you are making, share your experiences and bounce ideas off each other. You never know. You and your friends might devise an excellent idea for a joint venture!

Exploring new places and experiencing new things together can also help you feel refreshed and motivated to return to work with fresh ideas. For example, imagine having a childhood friend who shares your passion for cars and then starting a supercar workshop or car dealership together. It's worth considering. Spending quality time with your parents is just as important. They don't want your money; they want your time and attention. Helping your dad fix his car or cooking with your mom can mean more to them than any amount of cash. Remember the famous line from The Godfather? "A man who doesn't spend time with his family can never be a real man." It's not about money or muscles—it's about being there for the people you care about. When everything quiets down, the spotlight fades, and you can count on your family to be there for you, lighting the way.

Your family is all about love and connection, and even though you might think it's hard to impress your parents or relate to them, remember that they have been in your shoes. They care about you deeply and want to share their wisdom and experiences with you. Spending time with your siblings is also essential—they are your family.

Balance and moderation are essential in life. Think of the ocean—it is beautiful and awe-inspiring when it's calm, but when a tsunami strikes, it becomes a force of destruction. Just like the ocean, it is vital to maintain balance in all aspects of your life. At your age, it is crucial to remember the importance of education. Even if you think you don't need a degree to be successful, education lays the foundation for your future. Don't let side hustles or part-time jobs distract you from pursuing your education.

Let us summarize the importance of balancing social life, family life, education, and side hustles. Being well-rounded means embracing every aspect of life, including the human connections that make it all worthwhile.

Money can bring happiness. It is not, however, the only key to a fulfilling life.

Stay close to your loved ones, focus on your goals, and surround yourself with like-minded people. That way, when you reach the top, you won't be lonely but will celebrate your achievements with those who matter most.

Prioritizing Self-Care

The notion of self-care may come across as indulgent or non-essential, particularly when juggling a busy schedule that already feels overwhelming. However, to be clear, self-care is neither a luxury nor a sign of laziness. It's a fundamental aspect of human well-being, and it becomes even more essential when your time and energy are divided among multiple pursuits.

Physical and mental well-being are not just prerequisites for personal happiness; they are the scaffolding that supports all your other endeavors.

Burnout, stress, and health problems are not badges of honor—they are red flags that could severely compromise one's ability to perform well in school, work effectively, or grow your side hustle into a full-fledged business.

Ensure that you carve out some time just for you. You don't need to be busy all the time. Use this time to do the things that you want to do to reset. This can be going for a walk, watching a movie, reading a book, or journalling.

Managing Your Physical Well-Being

The old adage "Health is wealth" holds genuine wisdom.

Regular exercise is not just good for the body; it's a stress reliever that can enhance cognitive function. Prioritize a form of physical activity you enjoy, whether going to the gym, dancing, or even taking long walks. Nutrition also plays a vital role. Fast food might be convenient when you hop between classes, work, and your side business, but a balanced diet fuels the body and the brain more effectively.

It is essential to schedule your self-care just as you would schedule study sessions, work hours, or time for your side hustle. Mark out periods for self-care on your calendar. It might be a 20-minute workout, a half-hour reading before bed, or a weekend afternoon entirely free from commitments. If you don't schedule it, it won't happen.

Mental Self-Care: The Invisible Workload

In the race to be hyper-productive, mental well-being often takes a backseat. Yet, your mental health helps you sustain your productivity, creativity, and resilience. Schools focus on grades, part-time jobs focus on performance metrics, and your side hustle may be about growth and revenue. None of these domains explicitly reward you for maintaining good mental health, but they all implicitly require it. Mindfulness techniques, short relaxation exercises, and even structured "do-nothing" time can be powerful tools in preserving your mental space.

Setting Boundaries

The world won't stop demanding your time and energy. The onus is on you to set boundaries. This might mean saying no to extra shifts at work, declining social events when you need downtime, or even making the challenging decision to drop projects or commitments that negatively affect your well-being. Boundary-setting is not a one-time task but an ongoing practice requiring self-awareness and courage.

Efficiency Versus Effectiveness

There is a tendency to view productivity through the lens of efficiency—how many tasks can you check off your list? But what about effectiveness? Are you retaining what you study? Are you providing value in your part-time job and side hustle? Or are you just going through the motions in a sleep-deprived haze? Remember that your part-time job allows you to develop skills that will help you throughout your life.

High effectiveness usually correlates with high-quality self-care.

Building Sustainable Habits

Forming habits takes time and repeated effort. Make self-care habitual, like brushing your teeth or attending work and school on time. The more ingrained it becomes in your routine, the less mental effort it'll take to maintain it, freeing up cognitive resources for your other endeavors.

In the grand scheme of things, the young years are a blip on the radar of your life, but the habits you form now can echo into adulthood. By giving self-care the priority it deserves, you set yourself up for a balanced, fulfilling life, capable of handling academics, work, and entrepreneurial endeavors with aplomb. You are investing not just in feeling better today or this week but in the future. So, honor that future self by taking care of yourself today.

Spotting the Signs of Burnout

While young, you tend to feel invincible. You feel like you can cope with whatever life throws at you. But in a high-speed world that prizes achievement and productivity, teens today often grapple with academics, part-time jobs, extracurricular activities, and even entrepreneurial pursuits. While ambition is commendable, this intense juggling act can lead to mental and physical exhaustion, commonly known as burnout. And no, burnout isn't just an "adult problem." It's real; it's affecting younger generations, and it's crucial to understand how to spot it and address it.

Burnout shows itself in various ways, both physically and emotionally. You might experience constant tiredness that even a good night's sleep can't fix. Your grades might slip, or you may need to be more engaged in your job or side projects. A general sense of apathy towards things that used to excite you can also be a warning flag. Physical symptoms might include headaches, digestive problems, or frequent illnesses due to a weakened immune system.

You might feel detached, overly critical, or increasingly disillusioned. If you notice several of these symptoms concurrently and persistently, it's time to address the situation.

Hit Pause and Reflect

The first step to navigating burnout is acknowledging it. This is not a defeat; it's a valuable realization. Take a break from your usual grind to assess your mental and emotional state.

Reflect on your commitments: Are they aligned with your goals, or are you just skating through activities without purpose? The answers to these questions can guide you in reorienting your energies more constructively.

Prioritize and Cut Back

It is tempting to think that doing more equates to achieving more. However, spreading yourself too thin can have the opposite effect. List all your activities and commitments and evaluate them based on their importance and urgency. This exercise can reveal that some activities consume much of your time and energy without offering much in return for personal growth or happiness.

Seek Support

Burnout often carries a stigma that dissuades open conversations about it. But discussing your feelings with trusted family members, friends, or counselors isn't a sign of weakness. It's a mature way to gain valuable perspectives to help you manage your situation more effectively.

Incorporate Relaxation Techniques

Mindfulness practices like deep-breathing exercises, meditation, or even a short daily walk can help reset your mind and alleviate stress. While these might sound like adult coping strategies, they are universally applicable.

You are never too young to adopt healthy coping mechanisms.

Commit to a Balanced Routine

No one asks you to drastically drop your aspirations or scale down your dreams. Instead, the goal is to integrate these pursuits into a balanced life that includes adequate sleep, physical exercise, and leisure activities that rejuvenate you. These aren't just "add-ons" but integral components that enhance your productivity and well-being.

Review and Adjust Continuously

The journey out of burnout is rarely linear. There might be setbacks, and that's okay. The key is to maintain a responsive approach, continually assessing your well-being and making necessary adjustments to your lifestyle and commitments.

In today's hyper-competitive environment, acknowledging and tackling burnout is prudent and imperative for long-term success and happiness. The teen years are formative, setting the tone for adulthood. By learning how to manage burnout now, you are equipping yourself with a critical life skill that will serve you well in the coming years. The essence of this learning isn't just to survive your teen years but to thrive during them, setting a precedent for a balanced, fulfilling life ahead.

BONUS 1: Financial Safety

Unfortunately, many scammers are crafty, trying to get you to give in to their requests and scams! So, let's discuss how you can remain financially safe.

Let's get real for a moment. The words 'financial safety' might sound more like an insurance commercial than something you must consider now. But bear with me. Financial safety is the lock on the door of your future—neglect it, and you are leaving that door wide open for anyone to walk in and rob you blind. And while you might not have much money to your name yet, the financial decisions you make today can ripple into your future in ways you can't even imagine.

Why Financial Safety Should Be on Your Radar

First, let's tackle why you should even care. You are young, resilient, and full of aspirations. But you are also entering a world where online scammers can drain a bank account faster than you can say "TikTok." Today's digital landscape has made it easier for people to swipe your hard-earned cash or—even worse—steal your identity.

We have all seen those headlines—some unfortunate soul tricked into sending thousands of dollars to a "long-lost relative" in distress or investing in a "guaranteed get-rich-quick" scheme. But let's be clear: scams aren't just something that happens to other people or older generations. Think it's only the older generation that's vulnerable? Wrong. One survey found that young adults are the most susceptible to scams [1] 44 percent of people ages 20 to 29 lose money to fraud, more than double the 20 percent of people ages 70 to 79. Let's face it, the stakes are just as high for you. It might be a modest savings account, an emergency fund, or the beginnings of a college fund—money you have probably spent hours working part-time to accumulate.

Now imagine losing all of it, not due to an impulse buy, because you didn't take the necessary precautions. [2] In 2021, Gen Xers, Millennials, and Gen Z young adults (ages 18-59) were 34% more likely than older adults (ages 60 and over) to report losing money to fraud, and some types of fraud stood out. Younger adults reported losses to online shopping fraud – which often started with an ad on social media – *far* more often than any other fraud type, and most said they simply did not get the items they ordered. Younger adults were over four times more likely than older adults to report a loss on an investment scam. Most of these were bogus cryptocurrency investment opportunities. This age group reported losing money on job scams at more than five times the rate of older adults. Many college students reported being scammed after getting a message at their student email address. The median individual reported fraud loss by people 18-59 was $500 in 2021.

As you step into the world of financial independence, it's vital to equip yourselves with the awareness and skills to fend off such predatory tactics.

Know the Enemy: Identity Theft and Financial Fraud

So, what are we discussing here? Identity theft happens when someone takes your personal info to make unauthorized financial transactions. Financial fraud is broader and can include all sorts of tricks, from bogus investment opportunities to sketchy crowd-funding campaigns. And yes, even in this information age, scams are becoming more sophisticated and more challenging to spot.

Playing Defense: Be Smart, Be Safe

To protect yourself, start by checking your bank statements. And yes, I get it. Scrolling through a bank statement is less exciting than scrolling through Instagram, but it's essential. Look for weird transactions and report them.

Likewise, fortify your passwords. Using "password123" for everything is like locking a vault with a paper clip. Strengthen your passwords by incorporating symbols and numbers uniquely, and do not keep the same password for everything.

You should also be skeptical when you receive an email that you are unsure who the sender is. Move it to spam, and do not click on any links in that email.

Anyone asking for your personal info unsolicited deserves scrutiny. And finally, stay educated. Information is power. Know the latest scams and how they work. The more you know, the less likely you'll fall for them.

If Disaster Strikes, Act Fast

Unfortunately, if you become a victim, it's not the end of the world, but you must act fast. Contact your bank to file a report and investigation. They will likely suggest canceling your credit card, and they will issue you a new one. Inform the authorities and file a fraud report. Also, consider seeking legal advice. Review and update your security measures afterward to prevent a repeat performance.

The Art of Scam and Phishing Recognition

Scams are not restricted to dodgy emails or messages. Whether it's a phishing email posing as your bank or a fake charity asking for donations, scams have gotten more sophisticated. They can arrive through social media, text messages, and even legitimate-looking apps. The best protection here is skepticism.

Verify before you trust. Only click links or share personal information if you're 100% certain of the source's legitimacy. Be very cautious before you decide to make online purchases. Fact-check the website you are interested in by going to scam detector websites like www.scamadviser.com. This excellent website allows you to verify and even provide a trust score.

It is essential to take this extra step to avoid becoming a victim of fraud.

Online Transactions: Treading Safely in Cyberspace

Even though you may be fluent in online interactions, familiarity should not breed recklessness. When conducting online transactions, whether it's trading stocks or buying from an e-commerce site, always ensure the website is secure.

Check for 'https://' in the URL and look for the padlock symbol in the address bar. Never conduct financial transactions over a public Wi-Fi network; always use strong, unique passwords for financial accounts. Remember, cybercriminals prey on carelessness.

Be vigilant, and don't offer them an easy target.

Investment Scams: The Siren Songs of the Financial World

As you age, investment opportunities may start crossing your path. But beware of Ponzi schemes, pyramid schemes, and other too-good-to-be-true ventures. These scams promise sky-high returns with little risk and use funds from newer investors to pay off the earlier ones. If you hear phrases like "guaranteed return," "risk-free," or "get in quick," those are glaring red flags. Scammers tend to create a sense of urgency so that you act quick to surrender your money to them.

Research and verify an investment opportunity before diving in. Do they have a legitimate website? Do they have a physical building that you can visit yourself? Are they on the Better Business Bureau? Do they pass scam detector website checks?

Consult trusted adults, read reviews, and perhaps most importantly, understand what you are investing in.

Banking and Credit Card Safety

Regularly check your account statements for unauthorized transactions. Use account alerts to notify you of significant transactions or low balances. If you spot anything suspicious, report it immediately. Your vigilance is the first line of defense against financial mischief.

Insurance: The Financial Safety Net You Didn't Know You Needed

The insurance world is not just for homeowners or car owners. Types of insurance like health, auto, renters, and even life insurance are forms of financial safety nets. Say you crash your car or your rented apartment has a fire; insurance can keep you from plummeting into debt. Understanding how insurance works now can save you from harsh financial lessons later on.

It's easy to dismiss all of this as stuff for adults to worry about, but here is the deal: The sooner you learn how to protect yourself financially, the better off you'll be in the long run. Scammers don't discriminate by age; they are after anyone they can fool. Learning how to protect yourself now will build habits that last a lifetime.

Protecting Your Investments and All Things Legal

Watching your money grow as you delve into the investing world is exhilarating. But here is the thing: The thrill of potential earnings shouldn't blind you to the necessary precautions. Think of this as building a ship sturdy enough to weather the storms you will inevitably encounter.

We are diving into the less-discussed aspects of financial safety: protecting your investments, securing online transactions, and understanding the legal parameters that could impact your financial security.

It's all in the Details: Fees, Brokers, and Safety Checks

While you are excitedly tracking your portfolio's performance, remember to account for fees, which could affect your profits. This includes management fees, transaction fees, and other costs associated with your investment accounts.

Moreover, verify your broker's credentials. A reputable broker can be your best ally in your investment journey, while a questionable one can be a nightmare you never saw coming. Regulatory websites often have databases where you can check your broker's qualifications and any past complaints lodged against them.

Legalities That Anchor Your Financial Safety

Talking about legal documents like wills, trusts, and power of attorney to teenagers may seem far-fetched, but consider this: When you start earning and investing, you are not just affecting your present but shaping your financial future. The earlier you understand these aspects, the more prepared you will be. Wills are not just for older people; they are for anyone with assets, no matter how insignificant they seem now. Trusts can protect your investments from excessive taxes, and a power of attorney can ensure that someone you trust handles your financial affairs if you cannot.

The Takeaway

A stitch in time saves nine, and a little effort now will save you a world of trouble later on. You should practice these habits today even if you are not banking big bucks. Financial safety prevents fraud or theft and creates a robust system to weather uncertainties. As you enter the world of investing and online transactions, ignorance isn't bliss; it's a one-way ticket to potential financial ruin. The stakes are high but manageable as long as you are proactive about understanding and mitigating the risks involved. So, as you chart your course through the world of personal finance, ensure you build a vessel sturdy enough to withstand whatever storms come your way.

Financial safety is not a topic that gets much attention, especially for teens, but it is the unsung hero of long-term economic well-being. Start giving it the attention it deserves now. You will thank you in the future.

BONUS 2: Self-Branding for a Healthy Financial Future

Finally, we must consider the *future you*. This involves ensuring you present yourself exactly as you want other people to perceive you. In a world saturated with digital profiles, eye-catching resumes, and competitive job markets, standing out is not just a luxury—it's a necessity. You might be wondering what this has to do with your financial health. Well, that is what this chapter aims to unravel.

Self-branding is not just about creating a slick Instagram profile or a polished LinkedIn account; it's about strategically defining who you are, what you can offer, and why people should pay attention to you. In essence, it's about becoming your own best advocate.

Why does this matter to you, especially when you are still figuring out your educational and career paths? The answer is simple: Early investment in your personal brand can open doors to financial opportunities you might not have even considered. These could range from landing that sought-after internship that pays you regularly to finding freelance gigs or even starting your own venture. Your personal brand is a long-term asset that increases your earning potential while growing in value as you progress in your educational and professional journey.

So, whether you are looking to secure your first job or be the next teen entrepreneur, understanding the importance of self-branding could be your first step toward achieving your financial goals. This is less about counting dollars and more about making those dollars count.

Self-Branding and Financial Health

Your personal brand is, in essence, the impression you leave on others. It's what people think of when they hear your name. It's how you are perceived and, importantly, within your control. As you build a positive personal brand, you are also likely to create a network of contacts—people who know what you are good at, what interests you, and what you can bring to the table. This network can be the gateway to financial opportunities, from part-time jobs to internships, scholarships, and more.

For example, if you are passionate about graphic design and have made this clear through your online and offline branding. Teachers, family friends, or local businesses might think of you when they need design work done. This is an opportunity for you to switch gears and turn your hobby into a freelance business to earn more money.

Furthermore, your personal brand can also elevate your value in the eyes of potential employers. As you apply for part-time jobs, internships, or even your first full-time job, a solid personal brand could be the differentiator that tilts the scale in your favor. And guess what? Higher perceived value often comes with a higher paycheck.

You are building your reputation. You are taking the steps today to make you a compelling choice for tomorrow's sought-after, financially rewarding opportunities. This is a fascinating crossroad where self-branding and financial health meet, offering actionable steps to leverage one to enhance the other.

Self-Branding, Step-By-Step

Begin your self-branding journey with a comprehensive personal assessment. Take the time to identify your skills, strengths, and interests. What makes you unique? What do you excel at? This is the foundation of your brand, the essential elements that set you apart from your peers. Your skills are not just a list on a resume; they are your intellectual currency, and their value increases when they are well-communicated and understood by others.

Then, turn your focus to your online presence, the digital face of your personal brand. Whether you like it or not, employers, universities, and even potential dates often 'Google' you before making further commitments. What they find can significantly influence their perception of you. So, ensure your digital footprint reflects the brand you are trying to build. Clean up any contentious or compromising posts and consider what your social media profiles say about you. The internet is an unforgiving archive, and an errant tweet or an offhand comment can be enough to damage your brand.

While the digital realm provides a valuable platform for self-branding, real-world networking must be considered. Remember, your network is your net worth. Networking is more than just about handing out business cards at corporate events. It is about building meaningful relationships with people who can help you grow personally and financially. These could be your teachers, career mentors, or even friends with a knack for money management.

These relationships form an invaluable support system and can open doors to job opportunities, internships, and scholarships.

Building your brand online is all about the details. Social media platforms like Instagram, LinkedIn, and Twitter offer a stage to express your interests and showcase your accomplishments. A personal website can serve as a portfolio that gathers all your brand elements in one place, making it easier for interested parties to learn more about you. But remember, with great power comes great responsibility. Online etiquette is a crucial part of this journey. Professional communication, even online, requires respectful, coherent, and engaging communication.

Don't forget about the offline world. Public speaking engagements at school or community events can serve as a platform for you to share your expertise and elevate your brand. Networking events and mentorship programs provide real-world settings where you can put your interpersonal skills to the test and meet individuals who can offer you financial guidance. Engaging with a mentor helps refine your brand and offers firsthand financial advice that's often more valuable than any online article.

Your personal brand goes beyond the borders of social status and can influence tangible aspects of your life—such as your resume. A robust personal brand makes you a compelling candidate on paper and can give you an edge in job interviews. It's not just about telling your potential employers who you are but showing them through a consistent brand narrative. Entrepreneurially speaking, a robust personal brand could be the differentiator that attracts investors or partners to your business venture.

Your personal brand can become a ticket to financial opportunities, provided you cultivate it thoughtfully. It's an investment in yourself that doesn't cost much but can yield enormous returns.

The Do's and Don'ts of Self-Branding

The adage "any publicity is good publicity" could not be further from the truth. In this interconnected world, mistakes are not easily forgotten and can tarnish your brand and, by extension, your financial prospects.

Take the example of an ill-advised tweet or an inappropriate photo that goes viral for all the wrong reasons. It can close doors for you before they even have a chance to open. Employers and colleges these days do digital background checks, and an online misstep can seriously compromise your opportunities.

Another common mistake is inconsistency. Your brand is your story; like any good story, it needs a coherent narrative. If you project different images on different platforms, you send mixed signals about who you are and what you stand for. This can be confusing for those who are trying to understand or invest in your brand. For instance, if your LinkedIn profile portrays you as a business aspirant while your Twitter feed is filled with reckless comments, it creates a brand disconnect that could be financially costly in the long run.

Overexposure is another pitfall to avoid. In an attempt to be everywhere, you could spread yourself too thin, resulting in a diluted brand message. Just because various platforms are available doesn't mean you need to be on all of them. Choose the ones that align with your brand and focus on building there.

The goal is not to be known by everyone but to be unforgettable to those who matter to your financial future—potential employers, scholarship boards, or even future business partners.

And let's not overlook the trap of inauthenticity. The temptation to create a brand that you think people will love is real, but authenticity is critical. People can spot a fake from a mile away, and an inauthentic brand is a shaky foundation upon which to build any future—financial or otherwise. Authenticity resonates with people, and that emotional connection is what can attract the right kind of economic opportunities your way.

Building a brand is not a one-off exercise; it's a journey that evolves with you.

As your interests and goals change, your brand should reflect that growth. This is what we call future-proofing your brand. Like any other asset, your brand requires regular maintenance and updating. It means revisiting your online presence and real-world interactions to ensure they align with your evolving goals and interests. Your brand should transition with you as you transition from high school to college or from a part-time job to a full-time role.

Part of future-proofing also involves staying abreast of current trends and technologies. The digital landscape changes rapidly, so continuously learning new skills is essential to remain competitive. A blog might have been a great way to build your brand a few years ago, but today, podcasting or vlogging might be more effective. Your ability to adapt and evolve will keep your brand relevant, opening doors to new and better financial opportunities.

Furthermore, always seek feedback, but also know how to filter it. Not all criticism is constructive, and not all praise is genuine. Take what aligns with your vision for your brand and use it to make informed adjustments. Likewise, continue to network and engage in mentorship even when you feel your brand is solid. Remember, a brand is a living entity; it grows, learns, and adapts as you do.

As you step into the world armed with the knowledge and strategies to build a robust personal brand, remember that your brand is more than just a tool for financial gain; it reflects who you are and who you aspire to be. It is the legacy you will leave behind in every room you exit and every life you touch. While the immediate benefits of a well-managed personal brand may be scholarships, internships, or job opportunities, the long-term rewards are far more profound. You will find that a strong brand offers not just economic dividends but also social and emotional ones. It creates avenues for authentic relationships, mutual growth, and shared victories.

Share the Wisdom!

Money may not be a magical solution to anything, but understanding it has the power to transform your experience. With this knowledge at your fingertips, you'll be far less stressed out by money than many people, making you the perfect person to share the wisdom.

Simply by sharing your honest opinion of this book and a little about your own experience, you'll show new readers where they can find this essential information.

Thank you so much for your support. I wish you a bright and prosperous future.

Scan the QR code to leave your review!

Conclusion and Next Steps

Why am I sharing these budgeting tips and insights with you? I genuinely care and want to help you find success and happiness. I have chosen to write this book to guide you through these tough times and show you a world with many possibilities.

You might feel overwhelmed by all the pressures of fitting in and dealing with life changes. Remember to take things slow; relying on your strong support network is okay. They have a wealth of experience and knowledge to share with you. Be open to their advice, even when budgeting and managing your expenses. Be aware of the people in your life who are genuinely interested in your well-being. Sometimes, friends might be more interested in your money than your friendship. Be cautious and distance yourself from such people.

Finding balance and continuing your education is an art form. Applying this to your life is essential, even when it feels like a challenge. You have now learned the techniques to weave this teaching into your daily routine. Your parents have invested in your future, and it is up to you to continue and set the bar high.

Likewise, remember that discipline and focus are the keys to success. Work on yourself to continuously learn and grow to rise to the top. The world is rapidly changing, and only well-prepared people will thrive. Financial freedom and well-being are within your reach. Remember to practice budgeting and time management, no matter how much you earn.

Develop a habit of setting aside a portion of your income for the future by making it automatic. Learn from past mistakes from elders and aim for a successful life with discipline, effective budgeting, and healthy saving habits.

Also, cultivate gratitude for every dollar you earn and spend. Gratitude can be humbling and impact you and those around you. Embrace the lessons and experiences of those you admire and apply them to your journey. Throughout this book, we have explored various strategies to break free from being overwhelmed and the formula to achieve financial independence. While money is essential, it is not a magic solution. It can enhance who you are but won't fundamentally change you.

Wishing you a prosperous and successful life,

Your friend

Tammy Francis

References

1. Step 1: Adulting 101: The "Why"

1. Friedman, Daniel "How Much Should a Teenager Save from a Paycheck" Modern Teen, n.d.
   http:/modernteen.co/how-much-should-a-teenager-save-from-a-paycheck/

2. Step 2: Savings Made Easy

1. Amato-McCoy, Deena "Study: Teens Twice as Likely to Shop Online Than Adults" Chainstorage, 16 December 2017
   https://www.chainstorage.com/technology/study-teens-twice-likely-shop-online-adults
2. Puiu, Tibi "How the Subconscience and Emotions Drive Consumer Spending: Humans Make Decisions Based on Emotions, Not Logic", Zmescience, 18 March 2022 https://www.zmescience.com/science/how-the-subconscious-and-emotions-drive-consumer-spending
3. Elliott, Candice "8 Money Tips For Teens So Your Future Self Will Thank You", Listen Money Matters
   https://www.listenmoneymatters.com/money-tips-for-teenagers/
4. Varcoe, Karen P., PhD, Peterson, Shirley S., MD, RD, Wooten Swanson, Patti, MS, RD Johns, Margaret C, MS, RD "What Do Teens Want to Know About Money: A Comparison of 1998 and 2008" Wiley, 6 May 2010
   https://onlinelibrary.wiley.com/doi/full/10.1111/j.1552-3934.2010.00032.x

3. Step 3: How to Use Credit to Your Advantage

1. "FICOInsurance Scores Using Credit Data to Predict Insurance Loss", FICO Insurance scores, n.d.,
   https://insurancescores.fico.com/UsingData
2. Chase, Derek L., CPA, CA, LIT "Young Adults and Credit Card Debt", Bankruptsy Trustee BC, 11 May 2022
   https://bankruptcytrusteebc.ca/blog/young-adults-and-credit-card-debt/
3. De Matteo, Megan "The Average American has $90,460 in Debt: Here's How Much Debt Americans Have at Every Age" , CNBC, 14 November 2023 https://www.cnbc.com/select/average-american-debt-by-age/

Mid-book Review Page

1. "Famous Financial Literacy Quotes and Sayings: Data & Quotes." National Financial Educators Council. Last modified March 26, 2024.
   https://www.financialeducatorscouncil.org/financial-literacy-quotes/.

5. Step 5: Budgeting: Living below your means

1. Daniel Friedman "How Much Should a Teenager Save From a Paycheck", Modern Teen, n.d.
   https://modernteen.co/how-much-should-a-teenager-save-from-a-paycheck/
2. Barile, Nancy "S.M.A.R.T. Goal Setting for Students: The Smart Goal Setting Method: Tips for Setting Successful Goals With Students." Education Week, 20 January 2015, https://www.edweek.org/teaching-learning/opinion-10-tips-for-setting-successful-goals-with-students/2015/01. Accessed August 2021.
   https://www.asvabprogram.com/media-center-article/65
3. Sahadi, Jeanne "Many Parents Say They Are Still Financially Subsidizing Their Adult Children", CNN, 25 January 2024
   https://www.cnn.com/2024/01/25/success/parenting-adult-children-living-home

6. Step 6: Make More Money, Repeat!

1. Stawski, Benji and White, Alexandra "How FDIC Insurance Worksm Plus a Breakdown of Coverage Limits", CNBC, 29 January 2024
   https://www.cnbc.com/select/fdic-insurance/

8. Step 8: Time Management

1. Scroggs, Laura, PhD "The Pomodoro Technique: Beat Procrastination and Improve Your Focus One Pomedoro at a Time" Todoist, n.d.
   https://todoist.com/productivity-methods/pomodoro-technique

BONUS 1: Financial Safety

1. Lieber, Ron "The Young Fall for Scams More Than Seniors Do. Time for a Warning", NY Times, 25 June 2021
   https://www.nytimes.com/2021/06/25/your-money/young-seniors-scams-warning.html
2. Fletcher, Emma "Data Spotlight: Who Experiences Scams? A Story for All Ages", FTC.Gov, 8 December 2022
   https://www.ftc.gov/news-events/data-visualizations/data-spotlight/2022/12/who-experiences-scams-story-all-ages#

Printed in Great Britain
by Amazon